# *God Shows Up in the Valleys*

*my personal journey
with an incurable cancer*

*Lucinda O. Doherty*

To Taylor, my daughter and spiritual rock,
who encouraged me to write this book
and gave me the strength and love to keep going
beyond my capabilities.

And to Greg, my husband, who stood by my side through
the worst sickness imaginable, and who loved me, took
care of me, and made me laugh.

# CONTENTS

# Introduction

The following book is adapted from my journal, which documents my journey with an incurable cancer: carcinosarcoma of the uterus—that is, rare malignant tumors that consist of a mixture of carcinoma (or epithelial cancer) and sarcoma (or connective tissue cancer). I hope that this book is an encouragement to those who read it. I pray that it strengthens your faith and helps you to realize that God is in control and that total surrender to Him is so important to survive your earthly troubles and sufferings. My feelings are real and may be harsh at times, but I want to not only encourage other cancer patients, who can probably identify with these emotions, but to also help others understand what cancer patients endure. It may be graphic at times, so forgive me. I only want to be honest.

My journey started three years ago in the prime of my life when my husband, Greg, and I retired and moved to a lakehouse in South Carolina. Although at times this book may seem to indicate otherwise (you will read about a lot of depressing and hard moments), these past three years of living with cancer have actually been filled with joy! In my story, I share how God showed up during those depressing, hard moments in His providential timing and in His special ways to bring me out of the valley I was in. He would show up by putting a person in front of me saying the exact thing I needed to hear. He would show up in an email from a friend with encouraging words at just the right time. He would show up in a small gift to brighten my day. He would show up in my morning devotions, giving me the exact scripture I needed to read. And, most importantly, He would show up by giving me strength when I was weak or by healing me at certain times. In the most miraculous way, He would show up by not allowing things to happen, protecting me from things other cancer patients have gone through. God never forsook me during this journey, and He allowed me to find joy everyday!

My story or life testimony began fourteen years ago when I accepted Jesus as my Lord and Savior. At the time, I was not walking with Christ and was in my second marriage, to Greg. I have one child, Taylor, by my first husband, Dick, and two stepchildren, Sean and Nikki, by Greg and his first wife. When Taylor went off to college, she convinced me to return to church—and not just any church. She encouraged me to go to a Christian and Missionary Alliance Church, where they raise their hands and shout hallelujah! For someone raised in a conservative Methodist church (until I walked away from the Lord), this was very uncomfortable. Taylor insisted I go and told me I would understand within six months. About seven months later, I was sitting in church when the pastor began preaching on John 4 and the samaritan woman at the well. I suddenly realized that not only did Jesus know everything about the samaritan woman, but He also knew everything about me, and one day I would have to stand before God and give an account of my life. I knew then and there that I needed to be saved from my past and put my trust and hope in Jesus. Taylor and I were baptized together three months later (she had accepted Christ at a youth camp), and when she gave her testimony in the baptismal pool I discovered that she, too, had come to know Christ through John 4. It was then that I knew God is in control and has a plan for my life—and I was amazed by how much He is in the details. Only God could have used the exact same scripture to bring each of us to Him!

I then found myself in an unequally yoked marriage. Greg was raised Catholic, but he had walked away from the church at an early age. Greg respected my faith but wasn't interested in the path I had taken. He saw the change in me, and even noted that I was quite different from the person I was when we walked down the aisle together. God was actively changing me and sanctifying me. He had a very sinful person to work with, but I knew my sins were now as far away as the east is from the west. I began praying earnestly to the Lord to use me as a light for others. I found out during my first mission trip, to Chile, that my name means "light" or "illumination." I realized that God had given me this name for His purposes, and I began to pray. There are many stories I could share with you on how God has graciously used me as a light for others, but that would be another book!

An unequally yoked marriage poses many challenges, and I soon realized why God did not plan for marriages to be that way. One day when things were quite hard, I wanted to walk out the door and leave, but God stopped me in my tracks, showing me the scripture 1 Corinthians 7:20, "Each person should remain in the situation they were in when God called them." I knew then that God wanted me to stay in my marriage and that He would bless it. Greg and I have had a lot of great times, but we have also experienced our share of difficulties. Once during a difficult time, I prayed fervently for the Lord to please get Greg's attention. I yearned for him to know the Lord as I do. I asked God to do whatever it took, even if He had to take away our money. Greg's faith was more important to me than anything. God spoke softly to my heart, telling me that He would not take away our money because He knew how smart Greg was—Greg could easily find a way to make more money. Instead, God would do something that Greg had no control over. Two weeks later I was diagnosed with carcinosarcoma, a rare aggressive cancer of the uterus, with only a twenty percent chance of being alive in five years. And so my story begins…

# The Beginning of the End

# Before the Diagnosis

In February of 2015, a few months prior to my diagnosis, my husband, Greg, and I had returned to our home in Raleigh, North Carolina from an anniversary trip when Greg shared with me his desire to retire to a lake home. I was somewhat surprised because we had just spent the past five years renovating our home in Raleigh to enjoy during our retirement. When I thought of living at a lake, I envisioned driving down a long gravel road in the middle of nowhere, with no neighbors, and then swimming in a lake that was muddy and disgusting. But I felt that the Lord was encouraging me to follow my husband and that He would be with me. He reminded me that He is a fisher of men, and what better place to reveal Himself to Greg than on a lake while he was fishing. In obedience to the Lord and out of respect for my husband, I followed.

I set to work creating a process for us to find our new retirement home, and I made a list of the places where I thought we should begin our search. We had visited three of the five lakes on our list, none of which satisfied our checklist of priorities, when a friend recommended Lake Keowee in Seneca, South Carolina. Greg and I traveled to Seneca in June and discovered, much to our delight, that the lake and town ticked all the right boxes. We were so pleased with the area that we contacted a real estate agent and saw nearly twenty homes over the course of the next two days. We narrowed our search down to two prospective homes and left Seneca with plans to return the following week and spend longer periods of time in each home.

I prayed every morning that God would show us the right town, the right lake, and the right home in the right neighborhood. After we had returned to Seneca and spent several hours in each of the two prospective homes, we put an offer on the home we felt was right for us and were able to purchase it at a price we wanted to pay. The next step was to put our home in Raleigh on the market; it sold in four hours at the price we wanted. God's hand truly is in the details! As we were getting close to seeing our dream of living on the lake come true—just as we were reaching the top of the mountain, basking in God's blessings—I knew the valley would come.

We closed on our new home in Seneca and hired a contractor for minor renovations, which would take six to eight weeks. During those few weeks, we took periodic trips to Seneca to check on the progress of our new home. On one such trip, Greg bought a tritoon boat, and we spent the weekend on the lake with my brother, John, and his wife, Rhonda. And it was on this beautiful weekend that I first noticed something wasn't quite right.

While on the lake, I took off my cover-up and noticed that I couldn't hold in my stomach. I made a comment to Rhonda about how odd it was. I had been working out at the gym four to six times a week, and I was in the best shape of my life. But I brushed it off, chalked it up to old age, and let it go.

Our next trip to the lake was scheduled for Monday, August 17, but on Sunday evening I started bleeding. This, too, confused me because I had gone through menopause over twelve years ago. I assumed it meant that I needed a hysterectomy, so I called my doctor on Monday morning, left a message, and departed for Seneca. Two hours later, my doctor called saying she wanted me to come into her office immediately. I was already out of town, so we scheduled an appointment for the earliest I could come in: Wednesday afternoon.

# Day 1 – August 19, 2015

I went to the doctor on Wednesday for what I assumed was a minor health issue that would most likely require a routine hysterectomy. After my exam, the doctor returned to the room, looking grave, and said, "I believe you have cancer." "Cancer" was certainly the last thing I expected to hear. The word hung heavily in the air and my mind grappled with disbelief. I told her that I had just had a pap smear two months ago. Apparently, a pap smear only checks for cervical cancer. I had uterine cancer. When I asked her why I wasn't checked for uterine cancer, she said that there are no tests and the only symptoms seem to be swelling of the abdomen, unexplained bleeding, and loss of appetite (due to the swelling). I recalled the comment I had made to Rhonda at the lake when I couldn't hold in my stomach. I thought of my unexplained bleeding. I had uterine cancer.

As I was heading home to share the news with my husband, I felt peace come over me. The Lord reminded me that in this world we will have trouble, but to fear not, for Jesus has overcome the world. I would trust Jesus throughout this horrendous journey, trust that He would walk with me and probably carry me at times when I didn't have the strength to go on. I immediately knew that I would make it to the other side of this and that His glory would be known to many. I knew He would give me the strength to endure the pain and that He would comfort me when I couldn't take it any longer.

My doctor addressed the situation with a sense of urgency, knowing we were moving to South Carolina and what lay ahead of me. I was in a daze, not sure what path we were heading down. I did have a calmness from the Lord, indicating that He had this and not to worry, but I was still at a loss. My doctor worked quickly to schedule a next-day appointment for an ultrasound with a radiologist, and she contacted a gynecological oncologist surgeon to perform a biopsy. She knew I would need surgery, and she wanted me to see a surgeon as soon as possible.

The results of the ultrasound showed a large tumor inside my uterus. Four days later, the oncology surgeon at UNC biopsied the tumor, and then we discussed my treatment options. The oncology surgeon *felt* I had endometrial cancer, which is a slow-growing cancer of the lining of the uterus. The best treatment option would be a complete hysterectomy, so we scheduled the surgery for three weeks out, giving us time to move, unpack, and settle into our new home.

The closing on our home in Raleigh was scheduled for the morning of Friday, August 28. The plan was for me to take our cat, Benz, to Seneca on Friday where he would stay at a local vet until the move was complete. Greg would finalize the closing and then meet me in Seneca where we would stay at the Hampton Inn until our furniture was delivered on Tuesday.

While I was driving to Seneca on Friday, I received a call with the results of my biopsy. Sure enough, I had endometrial cancer, but the biopsy also detected carcinosarcoma cancer cells, which is a very rare and aggressive cancer of the uterine muscle. The surgeon said the good news was that he had detected both types of cancer cells; it would *not* be good if it was one hundred percent carcinosarcoma, since that cancer is deadly. He highly recommended we reschedule my surgery for as soon as possible. This was difficult news to hear. I wanted to talk through it with Greg, but he was delayed in Raleigh waiting for the check from the closing.

While I waited for him to arrive, I called my daughter, Taylor, told her I had cancer, and filled her in on all the details we knew so far; Greg was on his way but ended up in several traffic backups. I had some quiet time in my empty new house. I went upstairs, kneeled down, and prayed that God would bless our new home. I prayed that He would walk with me through this cancer, completely trusting that He would heal me. I believed God had a reason to allow this to happen, and I praised Him for what he would do through me.

"So if you find life difficult because you're doing what God said, take it in stride. Trust Him. He knows what He's doing, and He'll keep on doing it" (*The Message: The Bible in Contemporary Language*, 1 Peter 4:17-19).

Later that evening, I checked into the Hampton Inn. Greg finally arrived around 9pm after what felt like the longest day of his life. We went out to eat, discussed the news from my doctor, and returned to the Hampton Inn, exhausted from the emotional duress of the move and my health. That night, I woke up at 4am to Greg sitting on the side of the bed, crying. He had lost his mother to cancer over forty-five years ago and couldn't bear the thought of losing me, too. I told Greg that I fervently believed God would heal me, but Greg didn't share my faith. My prayer was that God would open the eyes of his heart during this time and that his faith would increase. The following day, we called the surgeon at UNC and rescheduled the surgery for September 8, the day after Labor Day.

On Friday, September 4, Greg and I traveled to Chapel Hill, NC for my pre-op appointment. It was a grueling day. We spent four-and-a-half hours driving there, three-and-a-half hours at the hospital, and then five-and-a-half hours driving home. During the appointment, I learned that the doctors had detected a third type of cancer: cancer cells in my glands. They wanted me to sign some papers to be a research specimen since this cancer is so rare, and especially since I had three types. I felt like Job in the

Bible. I felt like I kept hearing bad news instead of good news. I felt like things were being piled on top of me. Finally, I broke down in tears. Greg comforted me, reassuring me that we would get through this. And so again I chose to trust God and to stand on His promises. He will never leave me nor forsake me.

"So keep a firm grip on the faith. The suffering won't last forever. It won't be long before this generous God who has great plans for us in Christ—eternal and glorious plans they are!—will have you put together and on your feet for good. He gets the last word; yes, He does" (*The Message: The Bible in Contemporary Language*, 1 Peter 5:8-11).

The Sunday after my pre-op appointment, Greg and I were unpacking boxes when a neighbor came over to visit. God prompted me to share with her that I had cancer. In turn, she shared that she had had breast cancer two years ago but was now cancer-free. She felt as though her cancer had been a wake-up call from God, and she had grown closer to the Lord as a result. Through this neighbor, God showed me that His hand is in the details and that He is in control.

Two days before my surgery, I read this in my devotional, Jesus Calling: "My deepest desire for you is that you learn to depend on me in every situation." (Young, p.261). Yet again, God affirmed to me that He is in control.

The day before my operation, Greg and I drove to Chapel Hill, checked into our hotel, and waited for my daughter, Taylor, to arrive. The week prior, I had sent an email to everyone I knew, asking them to pray for me during this time and promising to keep them in the loop as I progressed through this journey. These people received update emails on a regular basis and became my faithful prayer warriors.

I was overwhelmed by the number of encouraging responses I received to the first email I sent. They not only strengthened me, but also showed me God's glory and how He was actively working in others. I read these the night before my surgery.

Sandra wrote: "I become more spiritual as I grow older, and I believe there is something for us to learn with every challenge and with every joy."

Cheryl wrote: "'The name of the Lord is a strong tower, the righteous run to it and are safe' (Proverbs 18:10). 'Cast all your anxiety on Him because He cares for you' (1 Peter 5:7)."

Shannon wrote: "I am praying without ceasing, my friend. We certainly don't understand God's ways, but we can rejoice that God is always there."

Another friend wrote: "I am reminded of a song, This Little Light of Mine—well I just want you to know that your little light is more of a stadium light!! You exude energy and enthusiasm, especially towards God and from God, and your not-so-little-light has made a big difference to those around you…because of you, my sons and I have found a church home where we feel welcomed and loved. About 6 months ago, they were both baptized and confirmed!"

I was blessed to know that the Lord was working in me and through me despite my cancer. He is Lord over my circumstances and, as another friend wrote, "What a joy to know that none of this surprises our Father, and it's in His mighty hands that I place you."

And from Taylor, my greatest prayer warrior, "Spending the day in complete prayer for you. He's got you, He heals, believe it!" Taylor sent me a pendant with the saying, *It is well with her soul*" engraved on it. I began to wear this throughout my cancer journey as a visual reminder to others that it truly is well with my soul.

## Day 21 – September 8, 2015

Tuesday, September 8 marked the morning of my first operation. We checked into the hospital shortly after 8am for my 10:30am surgery. I discussed an epidural with my pain management team; then Taylor and my pain manager prayed over me. I was wheeled off to surgery. I remember being moved to the operating table, having a mask placed over my face, and telling the surgeon to please remove all the cancer. The next thing I knew, I was waking up in recovery, feeling very groggy.

Apparently, I had been in the operating room for almost four hours, during which time Greg and Taylor both became concerned for me. A radical hysterectomy was performed, and the surgeon told me that they removed my uterus while containing the cancer within (by then, my uterus was completely full of tumors). They also took a number of lymph nodes but didn't see any cancer there. I had a tumor on the outside of my colon, which they cut to remove the tumor. My left ovary was also attached to the outside of my colon, so they had to remove another section of my colon so as to not cut into the ovary and spread the cancer. I also had several more tumors floating in my abdomen that were removed.

I had asked for no visitors my first night because we had a lot of information to process, but I was delighted when John and Rhonda showed up! I was up and walking the next day when my older brother brought my mom to the hospital. Over the next two days, I had many visitors, and on Thursday (two days after the operation) I continued to improve and to feel the peace of God. The Lord ministered to me through this verse, "May the God of hope fill you with all joy and peace as you trust in Him, so that you may overflow with hope by the power of the Holy Spirit" (*New International Version*, Rom. 15:13).

Several days later, as I continued to feel the peace of God, I woke up with thoughts of thankfulness. I journaled this: "I feel so blessed right now, first and foremost that I know in my heart that God loves me and He will never forsake me; His rod and staff comfort me. He has given me a peace in my heart beyond all understanding. He will see me through this! Second, I am blessed to have the best caretaker in the world, my husband Greg. He is by my side constantly and keeps me laughing, along with keeping all the nurses laughing! My love for him has grown so much through this! Thank you, God, for answer to prayer! Third, I am blessed to have the three best children ever. With Nikki and Sean's love and concern and Taylor's rock solid faith, we will all get through this. Taylor is a true witness and testament to God's glory. I couldn't love these kids any more than I do! They are the best! And their spouses, Brad and Lindsey! And fourthly, I am thankful for my beautiful friends! I had at least eight visitors yesterday and my hospital room looks like a florist! Even my ex-husband sent me flowers; I was very touched by that. Thank you, God, for all you are doing through me! I know you will give me the strength to get through this! It is well with my soul!"

It *is* well with my soul. "Friends, when life gets really difficult, don't jump to the conclusion that God isn't on the job. Instead, be glad that you are in the very thick of what Christ experienced. This is a spiritual refining process, with glory just around the corner" (*The Message: The Bible in Contemporary Language*, 1 Peter 4:12-13). I was anxious for the Lord's glory to be made manifest on this journey of mine.

On Saturday at 4am, I awoke with a pressing on my heart to give away all the flowers in my room. The night nurses came in at 5am and I shared my plan with them. During the last two days of walking laps around the hospital floor, I had noticed that many of the cancer patients had few or no visitors, I didn't see any flowers anywhere, and I had heard a lot of crying. The nurses thought it was a great idea and one of them, Courtney, delivered the flowers anonymously while patients were still sleeping. I was able to talk to Courtney, who is also a Christian, and share my faith with her. My other nurse, Sumol, who was Hindu, thanked me for sharing my heart with her. It is my prayer that the Lord used me to plant a small seed in Sumol's heart. I'm reminded of this verse, "Above all else, guard your heart, for everything you do flows from it" (*NIV*, Prov. 4:23).

On Saturday morning, the doctor said that I was ready to go home. The nurses didn't want me to leave; in fact, one of them told me that I was like the cancer poster child—she had never met another cancer patient who had the heart and attitude I had. I fully attributed my heart and attitude to the Lord. It was by His grace and for His glory I was progressing through this journey.

Greg had made a bed for me in the back seat of our pickup truck so that I could lay down on the drive home. The journey home was long and grueling. I felt every bump we hit in my belly. I wondered if we would ever make it home. When we finally pulled into our driveway, I knew we had made the right decision. There truly is no place like home, which makes me long for my eternal home with my heavenly Father.

We had nothing in the house to eat, so Greg dashed out to the store and picked up a frozen pizza. I was so hungry that I ate it without thinking it might be a bad idea. At 3:30am, I woke up with extreme stomach pains and vomited violently. I was so afraid that I would bust open my stitches and staples. Greg was my knight in shining armor as he held me, cleaned up after me, and put me back to bed. I finally got a little sleep.

On Sunday, I woke up in my own bed, had a delicious cup of coffee, and sat in my rocking chair by the fireplace on the screened-in porch. I thought, "Life doesn't get much better than this!" I had to give myself shots for thirty days to prevent blood clots, and giving myself shots took some time to get used to.

Later that day a neighbor stopped by and offered to make dinner; after the pizza debacle the night before, I insisted on something bland! She had been an OB nurse at a Catholic hospital prior to her retirement. I shared with her that I felt like God had been physically preparing me for this journey. I was in the best shape of my life and I was looking forward to a speedy recovery from my surgery. However, my recovery was not without its setbacks.

# Day 27 – September 14, 2015

I awoke on Monday (six days after my surgery) after eleven hours of sleep, feeling great. I was unpacking boxes—since Greg and I still had a bit of settling in to do in our new home—when I noticed a heavy discharge. I called my doctor, who said that the discharge was fairly normal. Soon afterward, I noticed that I hadn't urinated for quite some time despite drinking a lot of water. I called my doctors in Chapel Hill again, and they told me to go to an ER in Seneca immediately to be catheterized. Once at the ER, the doctor performed an initial exam and found a tender spot on my right side. This, along with all the discharge, prompted the doctor to do a CT scan to determine what was going on. The pain was becoming unbearable as they rushed me off to perform the scan; I asked Greg to please pray for me, and he did. He later told me that he feared I would die that night.

The doctor found a pocket of fluid and recommended we go to the hospital in Greenville in case it needed to be aspirated. At this point, the discharge I was experiencing had become a flooding mess. I was running a high fever, I was in extreme pain and discomfort, and I was becoming delirious and losing control of my bodily functions. At 10:30pm, I was dressed in Depends undergarments and hospital scrubs when I lost control of my bowels and needed to be cleaned up and redressed. It was such a humiliating experience, but I was humbled and extremely thankful for the nurses who so lovingly took care of me. Instead of an ambulance ride, Greg then drove me to the hospital in Greenville for admittance.

Greg and I finally arrived at the hospital where I was hooked up to fluids and antibiotics and got a few hours of sleep. The next morning, I met with a group of

22

gynecological oncology surgeons, who were happy to take me on as a patient and follow my treatment. I was very thankful that things were falling into place. Greg and I were both concerned that since I had my surgery in North Carolina and I was now in South Carolina some things might slip through the cracks.

Although things were falling into place, this episode of setbacks wasn't over. Later that afternoon, my right leg began to swell. The doctor feared I might have a bloodclot and performed a Doppler ultrasound, but my veins were perfectly clear. Then, when I stood up for the first time in quite a while, fluid began gushing out of me again—so much fluid that a nurse had to be summoned to clean up both me and the room! At this point, the doctors realized the fluid wasn't normal and supposed I might have a fistula. They ran a few tests, but the results were inconclusive.

I was frustrated by these setbacks and the fact that there wasn't a clear answer. I began reflecting on the craziness of the past two days, and the Lord showed me that I had been focusing on my negative circumstances. So instead, I chose to focus on the highlights: two great things had happened in the midst of that crazy day. First, my neighbor brought me flowers (they brought tears of joy to my eyes!), and second, I spoke with the hospital chaplain for over an hour, sharing my story with her. Afterward, she prayed over me.

In my devotions that night I read, "To him who is able to keep you from stumbling and to present you before his glorious presence without fault and with great joy—to the only God our Savior be glory, majesty, power and authority, through Jesus Christ our Lord, before all ages, now and forevermore! Amen" (*NIV*, Jude 1:24-25). I praised God for bringing me this far and I knew He would continue carrying me through this journey. I knew God would use this cancer for my good and for His glory.

The following morning I awoke early and read my devotions as I waited for the doctors to do their rounds. The swelling had gone down in my leg and the antibiotics seemed to have taken care of the infection, but there was still no answer as to all the fluid. Again, I chose to trust God; I chose to trust that He is Lord over my circumstances and that He is in control. He immediately showed me that He is not only in control, but He is also in every detail of my life—if only I would pay attention to Him!

That morning, another doctor, Dr. E. (from the oncology gynecological group), came in to attend to me. It turns out that he was the doctor who my surgeon at UNC wanted to refer me to for follow up treatment. Apparently, they knew each other from school and had done a fellowship together. My "new" doctor said I could go home that day, and he would schedule a follow-up appointment for the next week.

When I arrived home, I showered and prepared to go out to dinner. I was eager to return to a sense of normalcy, but that was short-lived. I received a call from my surgeon at UNC, who had the results of the pathology. The diagnosis was devastating.

Again, I felt like Job…things kept getting worse and worse. The results of the pathology showed no endometrial cancer cells—only one hundred percent carcinosarcoma cells, which is the aggressive cancer with a dire prognosis. The cancer was stage 3A (cancer extending outside the uterus, the fallopian tubes, the ovaries and into the pelvis area) and, unfortunately, there is little data on this type of cancer because it's very rare. The doctor wanted to start treatment quickly and aggressively; he felt he only had one chance to kill this cancer and had to hit it with everything they had. He suggested a sandwich approach: giving me two types of chemo drugs, Carboplatin and Taxol, for three rounds (every three weeks), then heavy external and internal radiation, followed by three more rounds of chemo. The prognosis? I had a twenty percent chance of being alive in five years.

The next day, the discharge began again. It was so heavy that I was going through a pad every fifteen minutes! The doctor told me to continue walking around the house. After all, the fluid had to go somewhere. Unable to leave the house, or accomplish much of anything for that matter, Greg and I called Taylor and told her the news I had received from my doctor the previous night. Initially, Taylor was upset that we hadn't conferenced her in, but we explained that the news came as such a shock that we could hardly process what was going on.

Taylor and Greg became angry with each other because they both wanted to be involved in my treatment decisions. Taylor, being my own flesh and blood, wanted to have input on the decisions, and Greg, being my husband, sometimes made decisions without thinking of others. I felt so overwhelmed. More than anything, I needed Greg and Taylor to work as teammates, supporting each other as they supported me. I was crying in the bathroom when a good friend from Raleigh called. Her timing was providential. I was able to talk with her about everything I was going through, processing and unpacking my experiences and emotions. Then, a neighbor brought over dinner and visited with me for a half hour. We chatted and laughed, and I was so refreshed to be distracted from my circumstances, even for a short while.

## Day 31 – September 18, 2015

I was still swollen the next day, but my discharge was back to normal. I called all of our family members and told them the results of the pathology report. The news was so shocking that I'm not sure how any of them took it. Greg and I craved a little normalcy, so we resumed our regular Friday night dates and went to a late dinner at a restaurant in Clemson. We ate late since Taylor and her husband, Brad, were coming in from New York and wouldn't arrive until nearly midnight.

On Sunday, Brad and Taylor took me to a local church. I felt an urgent need to get plugged into a church where I could praise God and have the support of local Christian friends. We met the pastors and a woman who lead a women's Bible study on Tuesdays; she invited me to come. Sunday was a day of restoration. I felt like I was healing and becoming stronger. I received an email from a friend with this encouraging scripture: "So we do not lose heart. Though our outer self is wasting away, our inner self is being renewed day by day. For this light, momentary affliction is preparing for us an eternal weight of glory beyond all comparison, as we look not to the things that are seen but to the things that are unseen. For the things that are seen are transient, but the things that are unseen are eternal" (*English Standard Version*, 2 Cor. 4:16-18).

On Monday, Brad flew back to New York, but Taylor stayed and worked remotely. I unpacked more boxes and slowly but surely our house began to feel more like a home. My body, too, began to feel more like a home. I could still feel the stitches in my belly, but I was feeling better and better, stronger and stronger with each passing day. One of my neighbors brought over chocolate (our mutual weakness!), and we walked through the neighborhood together. Later that afternoon, Taylor and I got pedicures together. My life began to take on a more "normal" routine.

It seems that after my stumbling block in the hospital early on, I was experiencing a miraculous recovery. On Tuesday, Taylor and I went to the women's Bible study at the church, and I met some wonderful women who have since become dear friends. As it turns out, one of these ladies had also had uterine cancer and was in remission. There are no coincidences in God's world! He places people in our lives at just the right time to be a blessing and encouragement.

Taylor returned to New York on Wednesday, but not before we were able to walk down to an outdoor church on the lake, where a huge wooden cross overlooks the water. It's a beautiful setting and one of my favorite places to be: at the foot of the cross. We held hands, had a good talk, and shed a few tears. After dinner that evening, Greg wanted to take me out on the boat for a short cruise. I hadn't been able to go out on the boat since my surgery, but the lake was so calm that evening we didn't have to worry about being bumped around by waves. We had hardly been out for ten minutes when the boat just died. I went into a panic. All I could think about was spending the night on the boat…stranded, in the cold, without a bathroom. Had I been healthy, I probably would have thought it was funny. Instead, panic set in. I called everyone I knew in the neighborhood and left messages. Within ten minutes, one of the neighbors called me back and sent out a rescue boat with three guys to tow us in. It turned out to be quite comical when it was all over.

Before Greg and I moved to our lake house, I had prayed fervently for God to show us the right house, in the right neighborhood, on the right lake, in the right town. He certainly did. God surrounded us with the most caring and

Godly neighbors, who demonstrated God's love in the form of dinner, neighborhood walks, chocolate, and a boat rescue. I felt truly blessed.

On Thursday, September 24, a little over two weeks after my surgery, I had a follow-up appointment with Dr. E., who said that I was healing very well. We made an appointment for me to return in two weeks and, if all was well, to start chemo in three weeks. He wanted to kill the cancer as quickly as possible. He told me to work hard at getting healthy since chemo would really put me through the ringer. He also expressed mild concern about starting chemo before my colon was completely healed because the healing process would slow down considerably.

During my quiet time on Monday, I felt so overcome by my circumstances. However, the Lord showed me that I need to be on the lookout for Satan's lies! I need to constantly resist him in Jesus' name so that he will stay away. I know that Jesus loves me and that He will walk with me through this valley and carry me at all times. This was my prayer: "Help me, Lord, to depend on you completely and not to listen to the evil one's lies. Help me to focus on you always! I know you have a purpose for all that I am going through, and I believe that purpose is to glorify You! Help me to fight the battles and to win the war. Help me to put on the full armor of God, to stand against the devil's schemes, to stand firm! I ask this in Your precious name."

On the last day of September, I read this in my morning devotions: "I am perpetually with you, taking care of you. [...] You need not fear the future, for I am already there. [...] Your future is in my hands; I release it to you day by day, moment by moment. Therefore, do not worry about tomorrow. I want you to live this day abundantly, seeing all there is to see, doing all there is to do. [...] Each day of life is a glorious gift, but so few people know how to live within the confines of today. Much of their energy for abundant living spills over the timeline into tomorrow's worries or past regrets" (Young, p.285). That day was a beautiful fall day, and I went out for my first three-mile walk.

On October 3, I read this in my devotional: "When many things seem to be going wrong, trust Me. When your life feels increasingly out of control, thank Me. These are supernatural responses, and they can lift you above your circumstances. [...] If you choose supernatural responses...you will experience My unfathomable peace!" (Young, p.290).

This truly ministered to my heart! I need to remember this not only on the good days, but also on the bad days. I need to continually praise Jesus and thank him for my circumstances. I know He is in control. Although this world may think of cancer as evil, I know God can and *will* use it for His glory. Thank you Lord for Your peace, Your comfort, and Your strength to walk me through this trial. As Oswald Chambers said, "The true test of our spiritual life is in exhibiting the power to descend from the mountain. We are not made for the mountaintops...those are simply intended to be moments of inspiration. [...] We are made for the valley...where we have to prove our stamina and strength" (Chambers, October 1).

## Day 49 – October 6, 2015

On Day 49 of my cancer journey, I had an appointment with Dr. E. He and my surgeon were on the same page as to my post-op treatment: three rounds of chemo using Carboplatin and Taxol every three weeks, then twenty-five days of complete abdominal radiation, ten days of internal vaginal radiation, followed by another three rounds of chemo. I was also to have a PICC line (peripherally inserted central catheter) put in the next day in preparation for my first chemo treatment on Monday, October 12.

Later that day, I was at my women's Bible study when I broke down and cried. Everything was really hitting me; I felt so weak and vulnerable. The women prayed over me and I felt like my burdens were lifted. I felt so loved by these women and by Jesus. Afterward, I went for a walk and talked to God about how scared I was. In my humanness, I weep when I am sad and frightened, but I'm reminded that when I am weak, He is strong. I'm not alone in this journey. That evening, Greg and I had dinner at our neighbors' and then took a sunset cruise, which helped to take my mind off of everything.

On Wednesday, I was up at 5am to be at the Greenville hospital by 6:30am for my PICC line appointment. It went smoothly, but it felt so strange. To put in the PICC line, the doctor inserted a catheter in my arm around my bicep and ran it through my vein up to my heart. This "line" is used to administer the chemo. The biggest inconvenience was that I now had several lines of tubing hanging out of my arm that I couldn't get wet, and I had to cover my arm in plastic wrap every time I showered. Needless to say, there would be no lake time for me.

Greg and I returned to Seneca and spent the afternoon on the boat. In the evening, we went to the country club to celebrate a friend's birthday, but halfway through dinner I began experiencing major stomach pains. I had cramps for over two hours and vomited violently. We were going to head back to the ER when I realized it was food poisoning from the chicken I had eaten. I prayed that my food poisoning was a precursor to the nausea that I might experience with my chemo. I prayed that through it God was showing me that the side effects from chemo wouldn't be worse than this.

Prior to beginning chemo, I went to have my hair cut short, per my doctor's recommendation. He advised that cutting it is usually less traumatic than losing it all due to chemo. Nikki, my step daughter, was with me, and when it came time to pay, the hairdresser said that the cut was free! Both of our eyes just filled with tears; I felt surrounded by truly compassionate people. I think that sometimes cancer brings out something special in people.

Monday, October 12 marked my first chemo treatment. The evening prior, I had taken six steroid pills at 6pm and then six more again at midnight. They're supposed to help with the nausea. I woke up at 5am, unable to sleep, so I spent time reading my Bible and praying. The first verse I read that morning was in Ephesians, "Finally, be strong in the Lord and in His mighty power" (*NIV*, Eph. 6:10).

I headed to the cancer center around 9am with Nikki and Greg, and the treatment started at 10am. It was a seven-hour process because they had to administer Prevacid, steroids, and Benadryl prior to the two chemo drugs. While I was undergoing the treatment, I picked up the new devotional Taylor had given me, *Streams in the Desert*, and read this, "When God lets us go to prison because we have been serving Him, and goes there with us,

31

prison is about the most blessed place in the world that we could be in" (Cowman, October 12, p.384). And, "If self-pity is allowed to set in, we will never be used by God again until it is totally removed. Joseph simply placed everything in joyful trust upon the Lord" (Cowman, October 12, p.384). Yet again, I was called to trust the Lord with my cancer and with my life. After my treatment, a neighbor picked me up and we went for a walk. I actually felt great, but it was due to all the steroids.

The next day I awoke early and spent a long quiet time with the Lord before my Bible study. I read this in my Jesus Calling devotional, "Take time to be still in My Presence. [...] Relax in My Holy Presence while My face shines upon you. [...] My Peace is an inner treasure, growing within you as you trust in me...circumstances cannot touch it!" (Young, p.300). After Bible study, Greg took me out to choose a wig, but I found myself focusing on my circumstances and feeling somewhat depressed. By purchasing and wearing a wig, I realized that I might fool people, pretending that I wasn't sick with cancer. How would God use my cancer if strangers didn't even know I had cancer because I was hiding it? I bought a wig but only wore it about five times; I wanted to be open about my cancer and decided to just wear a scarf.

Just as the nurses had warned, the third day after my chemo treatment was the worst day. I was told that chemo would make me constipated, but I wasn't proactive enough. During my surgery, my colon had been cut in two places and had only just healed. When I finally did have a bowel movement, I started leaking again. I felt like I would never heal. Achy flu symptoms set in and my legs hurt so badly I could hardly walk, but the silver lining was that I didn't feel nauseous, so I tried to focus on that.

From *Jesus Calling* that day, "Be prepared to suffer for Me, in My name. All suffering has meaning in My

32

Kingdom. Pain and problems are opportunities to demonstrate your trust in Me. Bearing your circumstances bravely—even thanking Me for them—is one of the highest forms of praise. [...] When suffering strikes, remember that I am sovereign and that I can bring good out of everything...accept adversity in My name, offering it up to Me for My purposes" (Young, p. 301).

Choosing to thank God for my cancer is a hard thing to do. It is a conscious decision to choose His trust and peace. However, this cancer has made me thankful for each and every day. Living with an expiration date has taught me to use my time wisely. This was my prayer: "Lord, help me not to get caught up in the busyness of life and to enjoy this beautiful place that you have placed Greg and me; I am so amazed at the beauty You have created. You have so much more to offer. You are a God of wonders."

## Day 59 – October 16, 2015

I was so excited that my brother, John, and his family were bringing my mom to visit me. It was her first visit to our new lake house and the first time I had seen her since I was in the hospital. Taylor also came in to town, and it was so wonderful having everyone here. Us girls went up to Highlands in the mountains where we spent the day eating, shopping, and having a wonderful, normal Saturday. But once home, I started draining heavily again. I shared my concern about a fistula with Taylor and how I didn't want to go back to the hospital. I went to bed that night reading in Colossians, "He is before all things, and in Him all things hold together" (*NIV*, Col. 1:17)

Everyone left Sunday afternoon. When my mom hugged me goodbye, she started crying and told me she prays for me every day. I hugged her, thanked her, and told her that God hears our prayers. Her response was, "I hope so!" I walked her to the car and told her not to worry, that God has this, it is in His hands, and that worrying is a sign of not fully trusting God. She is a constant worrier and even feels like it's her responsibility to worry, but I reminded her of Matthew 6:25, "Therefore I tell you, do not worry about your life, what you will eat or drink; or about your body, what you will wear. Is not life more than food, and the body more than clothes?" (*NIV*, Matt. 6:25). And "Can any one of you by worrying add a single hour to your life?" (*NIV*, Matt 6:27). And "Therefore do not worry about tomorrow, for tomorrow will worry about itself. Each day has enough trouble of its own" (*NIV*, Matt. 6:34).

Prior to my second round of chemo, I received a blessing in the mail: a beautiful handmade quilt from my best friend, Beth. It accompanied me to my chemo and now has a special place in my home. Just another blessing while in the valley. Several months later I received a beautiful painting of my grandson, Henry, and myself, that Beth's daughter had painted for me. This thoughtfulness brought tears to my eyes.

## Day 73 – October 30, 2015

I had my second round of chemo and was thankful that Sean and Lindsey were visiting from Colorado. Lindsey was pregnant with our first grandchild, due in December! She spent the day with me in the infusion center while Sean and Greg had some fun. I was determined to make the best of this cancer and to choose, with the Holy Spirit's help, to find joy every day. So even when I stumbled on the third day after chemo and went to bed sick, I found joy in the morning. His mercies are new each day. I found joy in seeing God do a mighty work—so evident from an email I received from a friend of Greg's. He said he wasn't a religious man but that he was praying for me every day! I found joy when I received a beautiful song from one of my daughters in Kenya, Ruth, with these words that I hang onto: "My God is awesome, heals me when I'm broken, strength where I've been weakened, praise His Holy name!"

My white blood cell count was dropping so I had to start getting a Neulasta shot after each chemo treatment. It works by helping the bone marrow regenerate white blood cells more quickly. Neulasta is a tremendous boost to the immune system, but it wreaks havoc on your hips. Because your hips are your largest bones, there is more bone marrow to reproduce the cells. In turn, this causes immense pain in your hips—pain that keeps you from sitting or even sleeping.

Finding myself alone and in the valley, I picked up my devotional, *Streams in the Desert*, and read this: "God selects the best and most notable of His servants for the best and most notable afflictions, for those who have received the most grace from Him are able to endure the most afflictions. In fact, an affliction hits a believer never by chance but by God's divine direction. He does not haphazardly aim His arrows, for each one is on a special mission and touches only the heart for whom it is intended. It is not only the grace of God, but also His glory that is revealed when a believer can stand and quietly endure an affliction" (Cowman, November 6, p.418).

I was so encouraged by this, especially since I had been struggling with my family members' reactions and responses to my cancer. They run the gamut from encouraging support to practically indifferent to outright anger. In particular, Greg and Taylor have been exceptionally supportive; they've borne the weight of this trial with me. Greg is not only an amazing caretaker, but he also has an outstanding sense of humor. He brings light and laughter to me daily. Taylor is my spiritual rock, always anticipating my needs and knowing what to say. My younger brother, John, and his family have also been supportive, visiting often and calling weekly to check on me.

At the other end of the spectrum, I've encountered worry and ignorance, fear and anger. My mom doesn't talk to me about my cancer for fear it might upset me. She prefers to keep it inside and just worry. My older brother doesn't know what to say to me or how to handle the situation, so he largely ignores it. My sister is angry about my cancer and becomes angry with me for not being angry about it. I know that everyone copes differently, but I also know that their reactions are not of the Lord. Their reactions aren't grounded in hope and the peace that passes all understanding. I've learned that it's best to acknowledge their emotions, but stay focused on God and pray that the Lord would work in their hearts.

I really needed my family to lean on, but through this, I realized that Christ is all I truly need. I'm learning to lean on Him and not my own understanding, to cast all my burdens on Him whose yoke is light. I will continue to find joy in this adversity.

## Day 84 – November 10, 2015

Mid-November marked two months since my hysterectomy, and I was finally getting to a place where I didn't experience physical restrictions. I was out of shape, but I finally felt like I could pick up the pace and start working out more seriously. My doctors told me that there's only a twenty percent chance I'd survive longer than five years, but I desperately wanted to be part of the twenty percent. I wanted to do my part to maintain my health while God was doing His part.

God's timing continually amazes me. His timing is perfect—far better than anything I could ask or imagine. In early November, I picked up yoga again to help ease my pain, stretch my muscles, and increase my strength. Somewhat surprisingly, I found an amazing yoga studio in Seneca and began attending classes. After class one day, I started talking to my yoga instructor and sharing my story with her. She said that she could tell I loved the Lord by the twinkle in my eye! Two other women overheard our conversation and began expressing how sad they were about my cancer. I think I surprised them with my response: not to be sad because I knew that God allowed me to have this cancer to work His plan through me.

Our conversation then turned to the meaning of our names, and one woman asked me what my name meant. Lucinda means "light." I suddenly had a flashback to many years ago when I had prayed every day for God's light to shine through me so that people could see Jesus. I realized that God was now answering that prayer in an unexpected way, but in His perfect timing.

When I choose to trust God, He uses me for His glory. Oswald Chambers wrote, "If you are going to be used by God, He will take you through a number of experiences that are not meant for you at all; they are designed to make you useful in His hands, and to enable you to understand what transpires in other souls" (Chambers, November 5). My deepest desire is that God would align my will with His and that He would use this cancer to make me more useful to Him. I'm constantly amazed at the opportunities the Lord has given me to share my testimony, and on November 10, I reached a point where I could truly thank the Lord for my cancer.

On this breakthrough day in November, I went to the dentist for an appointment, but due to my low white blood cell count, I was unable to have my teeth cleaned. Standing at the front desk, I began discussing fluoride trays with several women in the office—Amy, Allyson, and Terri—when the conversation turned toward my cancer and I shared the testimony of my journey.

Upon hearing our conversation, Rhonda (another office worker) came out of her office and began tearing up, saying, "Your faith is amazing! You shine with the light of the Lord." There is no other reason for my cancer than to bring glory to God. Soon, each of these women was shedding a tear and encouraging me. Terri told me how blessed she was that I had come in that day and how she needed to hear my story. After I left, I went out to my car and just sat there crying. I wasn't quite sure what had just happened, but I realized that God truly had a purpose for this cancer. As I was pouring my heart out to God, I began thanking Him for this affliction. When I returned home, I had an encouraging email from my friend, Herbie: "The Lord is working in your life despite the struggle of cancer and told me to read 1 Thessalonians 5:16-18, which says, "Rejoice always, pray continually, give thanks in all circumstances; for this is God's will for you in Christ Jesus." How appropriate for God to send me this message on this particular day!

The next time I went to the dentist, I found out that the office had been in an uproar just before my last visit. Apparently, everyone had been arguing and bickering over an issue, but the Lord used my cancer to shift their perspectives and to remind them not to sweat the small stuff. I'm so humbled that the Lord would use my affliction to bring peace and agreement to a dentist office. The Lord doesn't overlook a single circumstance.

Oswald Chambers stated: "We can all see God in exceptional things, but it requires the growth of spiritual discipline to see God in every detail. Never believe that the so-called random events of life are anything less than God's appointed order. Be prepared to discover His divine designs anywhere and everywhere." (Chambers, November 14). "I must learn that the purpose of my life belongs to God, not me. God is using me from His great personal perspective, and all He asks of me is that I trust Him." (Chambers, November 10).

## Day 99 – November 25, 2015

My third round of chemo was quickly approaching, and it was time to discuss my radiation treatment with my doctor. I was to undergo twenty-five days of external radiation in Seneca and then three internal radiation treatments over ten days in Greenville. The radiation oncologist discussed the harmful side effects of internal radiation with me, but he emphasized that killing the cancer was more important than any side effect I might experience. On the way home from my appointment, I broke down and cried. I felt like my life was nothing but a whirlwind of doctor appointments and treatments. This cancer was so aggressive and my body was in pain. But I had to celebrate the small victories. On November 20, I reached a milestone: my third round of chemo would be my last round until January 22.

After my third round of chemo, I needed a blood transfusion because my hemoglobin was so low. As I waited in the cancer center lobby, Christmas carolers came in to sing to the terminally ill patients. At first I thought it was sweet and thoughtful, and then I realized that *I* was one of the patients they were singing to. I began crying; I didn't want to be one of those patients.

My next appointment was with my radiation oncologist, and I had my body mold made to prepare me for abdominal radiation. The techs put crosses across my abdomen to help perfectly align each radiation treatment. Increasingly, Greg's and my lives were beginning to revolve around doctor appointments—quite an adjustment from a carefree life of retirement.

Wednesday, November 25 was one of the best days of my life! Taylor and Brad flew in from New York to spend Thanksgiving with both of their families. The morning before we were planning to travel for Thanksgiving, Taylor and Brad got up early and met me at the fireplace with coffee. We were sharing and just catching up when suddenly Taylor looked up at me and said, "Mom, God may have taken your uterus, but He filled mine!" With my sickness, I never thought I would hear those words! My daughter is going to have a baby! I am truly blessed! I have so much to be thankful for.

When you continue to ask God to use you as a light for others and to increase your faith, He will do it through the most ordinary circumstances. The beginning of December marked twelve weeks since my surgery. My healing was going well and I was running errands when I stopped at the bank to make a deposit. As I was waiting in line, the manager approached me and said that she could help me in her office. She could tell by my headscarf that I had cancer and she didn't want me to wait in line.

Once in her office, we had a delightful conversation about everything from fashion to how God was using my cancer to touch others' lives. Again, God ordained this meeting so that I could share with her the source of my strength and joy: God alone. I firmly believe that people will come to know and trust in Jesus by the words of our testimonies, and I'm humbled that He should use mine.

Just the next day, I went to Greenville for my nadir check, the low point of my blood counts. As the nurse was drawing my blood, I shared my testimony with her. The nurse had grown up in the church and had known the Lord all her life, but she had never heard a conversion story and was curious about how someone comes to know the Lord later in life. I was thankful to Jesus for putting my original testimony to good use!

Isaiah 55:8-9 says, "'For my thoughts are not your thoughts, neither are your ways my ways,' declares the Lord. 'As the heavens are higher than the earth, so are my ways higher than your ways and my thoughts than your thoughts'" (*NIV*, Isaiah 55:8-9). This scripture has always been special to me throughout my journey, helping me to realize that it's not about my plans. God has a plan and He knows what He is doing. His plans are better than mine; He knows what is best for me.

In this valley, we got the news that our first grandchild, Cora Layne, was born on Friday December 11. We were so excited. Greg left for Denver to visit, but sadly I was unable to travel due to my immune system. My sister-in-law, Rhonda, came to stay with me, giving me support and easing Greg's mind that I wouldn't be alone. While here, she helped me get my Christmas shopping done, which, by myself, would never have happened!

## Day 109 – December 5, 2015

Prior to my diagnosis, I had prayed for God to get Greg's attention and increase his faith. Two weeks later I was diagnosed with cancer. I felt the spirit leading me to explain to Greg where my peace comes from. By the fire one morning, I shared with him how I believe God is using this cancer to get his attention. It's amazing that God would use the very thing that had made Greg so angry (he had lost his mother to breast cancer, his niece had survived leukemia, and his step mother had survived breast cancer; needless to say, he was very angry with cancer) to hopefully show him what a loving and kind God He is. I believe Greg's anger will subside and his heart will be softened when God heals me.

As Greg and I talked, God gave me the words to say and I shared my faith with him and how I completely trusted God with this cancer. Greg listened and I prayed that, if nothing else, a seed was planted in his heart.

From Oswald Chambers: "Belief must come from the will to believe. There must be a surrender of the will, not a surrender to a persuasive or powerful argument. I must deliberately step out, placing my faith in God and in His truth. And I must place no confidence in my own works, but only in God. Trusting in my own mental understanding becomes a hindrance to complete trust in God. I must be willing to ignore and leave my feelings behind. I must will to believe" (Chambers, December 22).

## Day 136 – January 1, 2016

Greg and I enjoyed a pleasant holiday season with a family gathering at my younger brother's. It was good to see all of my siblings and to ease their minds of the pain of my disease. My older brother seemed to be dealing with the cancer better, but my sister was still having a hard time and acted as though she was in denial. No one really knows what to say to me or how to treat me. This was common throughout my journey, and I'm sure other cancer patients have experienced this. It happens not only with family members, but also with close friends. It's very difficult to know what to say to someone with cancer and withdrawal is a common reaction, which makes it a very lonely disease. After New Year's Day, I began feeling depressed. I was so tired of my cancer and the never-ending treatments. To make matter worse, in week three of my radiation I had problems with diarrhea to the point where I could barely leave the house.

However, while I was out one afternoon, a woman overheard me talking to a friend about how I was struggling with my treatments, and she asked if I had tried massage therapy. Then, she offered to give me a free massage! It was just what I needed. When I returned home that afternoon, I found a package on my doorstep from one of Greg's coworkers. I opened the package and inside was a hat, scarf, socks, book, journal, and several small items— all of which were perfect gifts for a cancer patient to receive. I was simply in awe of God's timing and providence.

Still later that day, I returned home from my radiation treatment and found another package: a baby calendar from Taylor's in-laws. I was so blessed. God knows just what we need when we need it. That day started out filled with depression, but God turned it around and made it a day filled with blessings.

In mid-January, I started to feel fatigued from the radiation. I was weepy and tired and could barely make it through a yoga class. I felt like my body just wasn't strong enough to continue the treatments. I could see how so many succumb to the pain and weariness of cancer treatments. I was reminded of this verse, "Blessed is the one who perseveres under trial because, having stood the test, that person will receive the crown of life that the Lord has promised to those who love Him" (*NIV*, James 1:12).

I am so thankful that God had prepared my body for this and gave me a strong desire to exercise and eat well. Without that desire, it would be difficult for me to get out of bed each morning. I had reached a point where I had to will myself just to walk. As I think about it, it's the same way with my spiritual life: I have to discipline myself and will myself to sit down each morning and spend time with the Lord. Though it may be difficult at times, I am always blessed when I do.

# Hope in a Time of Discouragement

# Day 156 – January 21, 2016

January 21 was another milestone! It was my last day of twenty-five external radiation treatments, and I got to ring the bell. The radiation techs told me that I had been a gift to them, always having a smile on my face when most of their patients struggled just to show up. I shared with them where my strength comes from and Who puts that smile on my face in these dire times.

My first internal radiation treatment was scheduled for Friday, January 22, but due to winter weather conditions, the hospital called and canceled my appointment. What blessed news. I had to do a bowel prep the night before and had an hour-long drive ahead of me...and my bowels were not yet empty! I was so thankful for even the small things. My appointment was rescheduled for Tuesday, which meant that Taylor, who was flying in on Friday evening, would be with me for my first internal radiation treatment. The Lord's timing is good, indeed.

In her infinite thoughtfulness, Taylor had planned a mother-and-daughter weekend trip to Highlands, in the mountains. This, too, was nothing short of God-ordained. We quickly packed and left on Saturday morning to drive to Old Edwards Inn. When we checked into the hotel, we received a free room upgrade to a suite with a fireplace. As we explored our cozy suite, we noticed three remarkable things.

First, there was a framed scripture in the bathroom, "Submit to one another out of reverence for Christ" (*NIV*, Eph. 5:21). This was the scripture Taylor and Brad had read at their wedding. Second, there was a framed scripture in the bedroom, "The Lord is good, a refuge in times of trouble" (*NIV*, Nahum 1:7a). I know that the Lord meant this scripture for me. Finally, as we left our suite to go for a walk, we happened to notice that our suite number was 1029—Taylor's birthday! Surely this is evidence that God is in the details.

Taylor and I spent Sunday relaxing at the hotel spa. I had decided to wear a stocking cap with my bathing suit since it was difficult for me to wear a scarf, and I hadn't yet reached the point where I was comfortable walking around bald. However, after I had finished my spa treatments, I was sitting in the quiet area (stocking cap off), enjoying the fireplace and waiting for Taylor to finish. I struck up a conversation with three other women and found out that one of the women had stage one breast cancer. She had already had a lumpectomy and had undergone three of her fifteen radiation treatments. In turn, I shared my cancer story and my faith with these women. I believe that the Lord used my story to minister to the woman with breast cancer, and I prayed that she would completely trust God in the midst of her trial.

Taylor and I returned to Seneca from our weekend away, and on Tuesday we went to Greenville for my first internal radiation treatment. I had been most anxious about this treatment, but I knew God had gone before me and prepared the way. I knew He would comfort me and give me the strength to get through this. He had brought me this far and I knew He would be with me until the end of this journey, and I looked forward to that day when I would be healed.

I adjusted my bowel prep medicine and made the one hour drive without a mishap. One there, the preparation for my first treatment was somewhat grueling. First, I was put in massive stirrups and numbed to be fitted for a cylinder. After the fitting, the doctor implanted gold beads in me, and I was moved to a stretcher for a CT scan. After the scan, I couldn't move for *two hours* while the physicists created my radiation plan.

Once my radiation plan was complete, I was wheeled into a small, claustrophobic vault just larger than my stretcher. At the foot of my stretcher was a machine nicknamed R2D2. The cylinder inside of me connected to a tube, which connected to R2D2. Based on the physicists' plan, a radioactive pellet ran from R2D2 up the tube and into my cylinder for internal radiation. Thankfully, once I had been fitted for my cylinder and my radiation plan had been created, the internal radiation treatment only took ten minutes.

Three days later, I returned to Greenville for my second internal radiation treatment. As I was speaking with one of the nurses about my faith, the physicist overheard me and asked what my "rock" was. I boldly shared that my rock is Jesus Christ and that He is giving me the strength to walk through this journey. I can't emphasize enough how thankful I am that the Lord would choose to use me for His glory. My heart leapt at the chance to share my faith with the physicist, and I pray that I planted a seed in her heart!

Fast-forward a few days to my final internal radiation treatment. The final treatment went perfectly; I rang the bell and cried tears of joy. I was five pounds lighter due to my four bowel preps. I shared with my doctor and nurse what a blessing they had been to me throughout this leg of my journey. This was the prayer I had journaled: "Thank you, God, for keeping me strong; thank you for comforting me and thank you for healing me." And so, I continued to stand firm on His promises. I continued to choose trust and peace over fear and worry.

I had an "end of radiation" celebratory lunch with all the ladies in my neighborhood. But I didn't want the celebration to be about me—I wanted it to be about God's faithfulness and His perfect plan. I shared with the ladies how, before Greg and I moved to Seneca, I had prayed that God would show us the right house in the right neighborhood. He did. The Lord had surrounded me with an army of supportive women, and I was so thankful for each one of them.

I was reminded of this verse in Isaiah, "In that day you will say: 'Give praise to the Lord, proclaim His name; make known among the nations what He has done, and proclaim that His name is exalted. Sing to the Lord, for He has done glorious things; let this be known to all the world'" (*NIV*, Isa. 12:4-5). I was also reminded of this verse in Matthew, "In the same way, let your light shine before others, so they may see your good deeds and glorify your Father in heaven" (*NIV*, Matt. 5:16).

When I returned home I received a beautiful necklace in the mail from my friend Kristin in Santa Barbara. I wore it and shared its meaning with my radiation oncologist. The necklace was actually named "Lucinda"; it had several blue stones, representing me, and one white stone, representing God watching over me.

# Day 174 – February 8, 2016

As I recovered from internal radiation, I was so thankful to Jesus for carrying me on the days I couldn't carry myself. I read the following (very fitting passage) in my devotional, *Streams in the Desert*: "Never look ahead to the changes and challenges of this life in fear. Instead, as they arise, look at them with the full assurance that God, whose you are, will deliver you out of them. Hasn't He kept you safe up to now? So hold His loving hand tightly, and He will lead you safely through all things. And when you cannot stand, He will carry you in His arms. Do not look ahead to what may happen tomorrow" (Cowman, February 8, p.65). It is all too easy to look at life's challenges with fear and trepidation. The Lord is constantly reminding me to choose him. To trust him. To let Him carry me.

On February 18, I went to the doctor for a follow up appointment, during which Dr. E. said that I was healing well and that I would be starting the first of my last three rounds of chemo the next Friday. After my appointment, Greg and I had plans to go out to eat, but he complained of stomach problems so we hurried home instead. When we walked into the house, I found a baby bassinet in the living room. Somewhat confused, I glanced around the room and noticed someone crouching in the stairwell—I realized it was Lindsey, our daughter-in-law. I ran to the bassinet and much to my delight found our granddaughter, baby Cora, inside!

It was my first time meeting Cora since I hadn't been able to travel to Denver when she was born. I held her all evening long. Together, Greg and Lindsey had coordinated this sweet surprise. In fact, Greg had even gone shopping and bought all the baby things Lindsey and Cora would need during their stay. This delightful surprise was Greg's 20ᵗʰ anniversary gift to me. I couldn't imagine a better gift than to hold my first grandchild in my arms!

In light of everything going on, I hadn't spent quiet time with the Lord in a week. I was in two Bible studies at the time, but neither seemed to fill my heart with what I needed in this season of life. The ladies in the neighborhood started a bunco club, but I decided not to commit to it since I was already feeling overwhelmed and stressed by the busyness of life. I didn't want to start filling my days with too much "stuff" and not spending alone time with the Lord. Life is too short for that!

I know that when I don't spend time alone with the Lord, it shows in my attitude. It manifests itself as frustration toward those around me, and it prevents His light from shining through me. As I have gotten stronger, I have relied less on the Lord and more on my own strength. The Lord reminded me that everything is possible *only by and through Him*. This was my prayer: "If I have to stay weak to stay close to you, so be it! Have your way with me, Lord. Let Your light always shine in and through me. Use me for your glory!"

From *Streams in the Desert*: "Earnestly desire to get alone with God. If we neglect to do so, we not only rob ourselves of blessings but rob others as well, since we will have no blessing to pass on to them. It may mean that we do less outward, visible work, but the work we do will have more depth and power" (Cowman, February 27, p.92).

# Day 198 – March 3, 2016

I love it when the Lord speaks to others and affirms what He has been speaking to me. On March 3, I received a message from my son-in-law, Brad, saying, "As I was praying over you this morning and specifically about your cancer, I felt that it has left you. I am so happy you aren't feeling bad after this chemo cycle." I cried tears of joy. I was so happy that God was speaking to Brad about my healing. Even though I have felt His healing from day one, it is so encouraging to see God reinforce that through others. God truly is a God of miracles.

That same day, Taylor had sent out an email saying that she was riding in Cycle for Survival, a charity bike ride in New York to raise money for rare cancer research at Memorial Sloan Kettering. As I read her story and why she was riding, my heart was overwhelmed with emotion. Taylor was doing this in honor of me—and she was five months pregnant!

The next morning I read John 11:4, which has become my go-to scripture whenever I feel down. This is the story of Lazarus becoming sick and eventually dying. "When he heard this, Jesus said, 'This sickness will not end in death. No, it is for God's glory so that God's Son may be glorified through it'" (*NIV*, John 11:4). After reading this, I was reassured that my sickness is for God's glory and that it will not end in death.

In mid-March, my healing was going well and I was feeling stronger. I even felt strong enough to volunteer for a day, so I volunteered with Stop for Hunger, which packages meals to be sent all around the world to feed the hungry. Several churches came together to work and we packaged over 50,000 meals in four hours. It felt so good to take my mind off of my situation and circumstances and do something for others. It made me think about returning to Africa to do short-term mission work again with Freedom Global. I've been to Kenya three times with this organization to help the poorest of the poor by opening a girl's school, creating jobs, and sharing the Gospel. My dream was to return to Kenya and see one of my Kenyan daughters graduate from college in October 2018.

When I returned home from volunteering, I received in the mail a beautiful handmade card from my special daughters in Kenya with two handmade angels inside. They had all written me special messages of love and encouragement. I am so thankful for Lydiah, Ruth, and Teresia; their faith is strong and I receive many encouraging emails from them. I truly pray I can return to Kenya to see them.

I was reminded in an email from my friend Debbie that valleys are special places to dwell in when we have to. It seems that every time I am dwelling in the valley, God shows up. He has been with me in the depths and has held me close! It is easy to dwell on the mountaintops and praise God, but it's so important to praise Him in the valleys, where He truly shows up. Pray for those you know who may be in valleys in their lives; pray for God to show up and walk with them. He is there and He hears you.

I have also been recently blessed by a new friend, Maureen, who I met at yoga. We had lunch one day and spent time getting to know each other. Her daughter passed away from brain cancer several years ago, and Maureen has been so loving and supportive of me. As difficult as it is to deal with my cancer, I can't imagine losing a child to cancer. Maureen is a strong and brave woman, and I knew God was using her strength and compassion to minister to me; and I believed my strength in the Lord ministered to her.

# Day 222 – March 27, 2016

Toward the end of March, I began to feel troubled again because I wasn't spending as much time with the Lord. When I fail to spend time with the Lord, I feel like my life becomes somewhat meaningless. It's easy for me to fall back into my old habits and then life suddenly spirals downhill. I yearned to be around strong, faithful people who would lift me up and encourage me. I needed the Lord's strength to continue to be a light for others.

I read in my *Jesus Calling* devotional: "Nothing is more important than spending time with Me...I do my best work within you: transforming you by the renewing of your mind. If you skimp on this time with me, you may plunge headlong into the wrong activities, missing the richness of what I have planned for you" (Young, p.90). This devotional spoke to me. I could see how I was falling back into my pattern of doing too much and being too busy. I was so excited to have my energy back, but I also wanted to find the right balance and not take time away from the Lord. I know that the Lord is my strength and apart from Him I am nothing.

After my quiet time with the Lord, I went to a difficult yoga class, worked in the yard, mowed the grass for the first time, and walked five miles. Then I spent the afternoon running errands. I went to Smith's Upholstery to see about getting cushions made for the kitchen window seat. While at the upholstery store, I met the owner and quickly realized that she was a prayer warrior. I observed as customers came in, sharing either good news or bad news with her. She always praised the Lord for the good news and added those with bad news to her prayer list.

I relayed my cancer story to the owner and asked if she would add me to her prayer list. I found out that the owner's dad had had cancer. He underwent eleven chemo treatments and is now doing great. I spent two hours there, getting my estimate and sharing stories. Then, I went to the Home Store to select tile for our downstairs screened in porch. Nancy at the Home Store remembered me from last summer and guessed I had cancer based on my headscarf. I shared my story with Nancy, all the while giving glory to God. I love these moments more than anything else—when I can share my faith in Jesus and the trust that I have in Him for my healing and strength. I had such a busy day, but thankfully it all started with spending time with the Lord.

Taylor flew in for a visit during the first weekend in April and we had such a sweet time together. Some of the ladies from my Bible study threw her a surprise baby shower; Taylor and I were both overwhelmed by their thoughtfulness and generosity.

# Day 234 – April 8, 2016

Back in March during my fifth chemo treatment, the Lord had placed it on my heart to do something special for my nurses and the other patients on my last day of chemo, which was now three weeks away. After all, my last chemo treatment fell on my birthday, so we might as well celebrate! In preparation for my sixth and final chemo treatment, I bought cookies and balloons. I printed several of my favorite scriptures and attached them to individual bags of cookies, praying that the scriptures would touch someone.

Friday, April 8, I woke up early and gathered everything I wanted to take to the infusion center: the baby afghan I was knitting for Baby Bubs (as we affectionately referred to Taylor's unborn boy), the gifts for the nurses, and the cookies and balloons for the other patients. When I got to the cancer center, I gave gifts to my three nurses and shared with them how much they meant to me. I gave April, my personal chemo nurse and dear friend, a pendant like the one I had been wearing—the one Taylor had given to me with the inscription, *"It is well with her soul."* I truly believe my nurses have been my angels throughout this journey.

I put the bags of cookies and the balloons on the counter and asked the nurses to tell the patients to take one and enjoy. A patient sitting beside me had taken a bag of cookies and, when he saw the attached scripture, he asked whose idea it was to hand out cookies. I told him the idea was mine and that I was hoping to bless others through my cancer. He loved it.

Then, I saw a young girl having her blood drawn; she was anxious to know the results of her blood test and to find out if she had cancer. I handed a bag of cookies to her and she teared up after reading the attached scripture. She had needed that verse! I then began carrying the basket of cookies around and offering them to those who hadn't taken any. One man took a bag, read the scripture (Philippians 4:13, "I can do all things through Him who gives me strength."), and told me that was his favorite verse! I was so thankful that God used me to bless other patients on my last day of chemo.

The day was winding down and Greg arrived to pick me up. It was time to ring the bell and say my goodbyes to my chemo nurses, April and Carolyn. Everyone clapped and celebrated with me when I rang the bell. It was such a special moment. I thought I was through and healed.

# Day 240 – April 14, 2016

In mid-April, I received a text message from my daughter-in-law, Lindsey, who lives in Denver. A group of people in Denver had been praying for me, and one of Lindsey's friends received this scripture while she was praying: "Just then a woman who had been subject to bleeding for twelve years came up behind him and touched the edge of his cloak. She said to herself, 'If I only touch his cloak, I will be healed.' Jesus turned and saw her. 'Take heart, daughter,' he said, 'your faith has healed you.' And the woman was healed at that moment" (*NIV*, Matt. 9:20-22).

I have always believed that my faith has healed me, and it is so encouraging when the Lord affirms it through others. Not long after I received this encouragement from Lindsey, I woke up on Sunday with pain in my abdomen. I went to church, but the pain was so severe I felt like I was going to pass out. I began to doubt that I was healed. And as doubt crept into my mind, sadness followed.

I quickly realized that those thoughts were not of the Lord but of the devil. The devil is conniving and plants seeds of doubt in our minds that quickly grow into gardens of sadness and depression. Recognizing the devil's tactics is of the utmost importance. I prayed for the devil to flee in Jesus' name and for the pain to end. And guess what? The pain ended immediately! God is good.

Two days later, I read the following by Oswald Chambers during my morning devotions: "You may have just victoriously gone through a great crisis, but now be on alert about the things that may appear to be the least likely to tempt you. Beware of thinking that the areas of your life where you have experienced victory in the past are now the least likely to cause you to stumble and fall. [...] Do not try to predict from where the temptation will come; it is the least likely thing that is the real danger. It is in the aftermath of a great spiritual event that the least likely things begin to have an effect. [...] You have remained true to God under great and intense trials—now beware of the undercurrent...stay alert; keep your memory sharp before God" (Chambers, April 19).

As I continued to heal and regain my health, I knew that I needed to be on the lookout for temptation. Satan was putting doubts in my mind about being healed. I was experiencing pain in unusual places, which was causing me to think I had new tumors. Several people approached me and tried to convince me to go to a healing service. But I knew that I had already been healed in Jesus' name. What more did I need? I only needed to recognize the devil's lies and claim healing in His name.

I was reminded of James 1:6, "But when you ask, you must believe, and not doubt, because the one who doubts is like a wave of the sea, blown and tossed by the wind" (*NIV*, James 1:6). The Lord continued to pull me back to His Word and His promptings. I praised God for yet another opportunity to use this cancer for His glory as I had the chance to share about doubting to others. I am also reminded of the story in Mark 9 when the disciples could not heal the young boy with convulsions. When the boy's father asked Jesus to help him "if he can," Jesus responded, "If I can? Everything is possible for the one who believes." Immediately, the boy's father exclaimed, "I do believe; help me with my unbelief!"(*NIV*, Mark 9:23-24). Jesus has used my cancer to strengthen my faith, and during the times when I've felt doubt, I have cried out to the Lord to help me with my unbelief, and He does.

# Day 254 – April 28, 2016

Thursday, April 28—the day I find out whether or not I am cancer free! I have dealt with cancer for 254 days. I have undergone one major operation, six months of intense chemo, and internal and external radiation. Most importantly, I wouldn't trade those 254 days for anything. I truly believe that God used me the way He intended to and that He received all the glory.

It was official: I was in remission. Or so we all thought. My CT scan looked good, showing no signs of tumors. The doctor expressed concern regarding a strange sac of lymphatic fluid, but we scheduled an appointment two weeks out to do a biopsy to drain the fluid and make sure there were no cancer cells.

Moving forward, I would have a CT scan every three months as well as follow-up bloodwork in three months to detect if the cancer was returning. There was a sixty percent chance of the cancer returning within two years.

Still, I was elated because I thought I was in remission. I sent out an email to my prayer warriors declaring that I was healed in Jesus' name. I prayed fervently that the Lord would continue to use me for His glory and never let me go. On the day I received my cancer diagnosis eight months ago, the Lord had laid it on my heart not to worry. Not once did I lose a night's sleep worrying about my cancer. I knew that God was in control.

The next day, I took off on a road trip to Amherst, VA to visit my girlfriends from high school. This was my first solo trip since my diagnosis, and Greg was concerned because I hadn't driven much over the past several months. Honestly, I was concerned, too, but I knew I needed to do it. I needed to feel normal again.

I spent the night with my best friend, Beth, who I hadn't seen in eight years! Beth and I reunited with a group of girls from our high school graduating class. We try to get together annually for lunch, but we had lost track of time and somehow eight years had slipped by since our last lunch. Most of the women were on my prayer list, so they knew what I had gone through over the course of the past year. They were all so thankful to Jesus that I had been healed.

I left Amherst late Saturday and drove to West End, NC to spend the night with my brother, John. Then I returned to Seneca around dinnertime on Sunday evening. I was tired out, but so content that I had made the trip.

# Day 259 – May 3, 2016

I began the first week of May with high spirits and plans to fly to New York City to co-host Taylor's baby shower on Saturday, May 7. However, the Tuesday prior I awoke at 4am with a 102-degree fever. After taking ibuprofen to help break the fever, I stayed in bed to rest. I felt like I had the flu, but I was fairly certain I hadn't been exposed to anyone with the flu virus. When I couldn't break the fever, I called my family doctor, scheduled an appointment for the following morning, and continued to battle with the chills and my spiked temperature. At my appointment the next morning, I was checked for the flu, but the test came back negative, so the PA briefly examined and released me. Sensing something wasn't right, the PA called me while I was on my way home and told me not to eat anything and to return that afternoon for a CT scan.

Two hours after the scan, the PA called again and told me to go to the emergency room in Greenville immediately. Apparently, the scan showed an infected cyst (the same pocket of fluid Dr. E. had noted) in my lower abdomen, which was the cause of my severe fever. And so began one of the most difficult hospital visits I had yet to experience.

Per the PA's orders, I immediately went to the emergency room, where I spent several hours while the doctors ran tests. I was finally admitted to the hospital at midnight, but because no rooms were available, I was placed in a holding room the size of a large closet with no windows. Greg had, of course, been present for the entire, hours-long ordeal. So when I was finally admitted to the hospital and placed in the closet-like holding room (where there was clearly no room for Greg to stay with me), I encouraged him to go home to rest.

When Greg arrived home from the emergency room late that Wednesday night, he realized that our cat, Benz, was dying. Prior to moving to the lake, Benz had become very sick with renal disease. He had survived the move but was slowly declining in health; the veterinarians had done all they could. He had been so sick recently that Greg and I had been discussing where we would bury him when he passed away. On that Wednesday night, Greg gently scooped up Benz and held him for several hours while he purred in his arms. Then, when he thought Benz was nearing the end, he wrapped him in a towel (in case he lost control of his bowels) and continued to hold him to the very end. Greg buried him the following morning prior to coming back to the hospital.

I slept fitfully that Wednesday night. My "room" didn't have a bathroom and the nurses' station was right outside my door, so I heard noise all night long. I was wide awake when Greg called early Thursday morning with the news of Benz's death. We both cried over the phone. But I knew it was an answer to prayer that Benz passed away while I was in the hospital; I think the Lord knew that I couldn't have borne to watch him die. When Dr. E. walked in at 7am, Greg and I were still on the phone crying; from the start, this day seemed to be spiraling down into a valley.

As my hospital stay progressed, my plans to fly to New York on Saturday quickly dissipated and I canceled my flight. Little did I know it was about to get much worse. To remedy the infection and release the fluid from the cyst, Dr. E. inserted a drain and attached a Bellows pump. The prognosis? I would have to stay in the hospital for three days while the fluid was pumped out. The only piece of good news was that I was transferred out of my closet-like holding cell to an actual room.

On Friday, things took a turn for the worse yet again. My stomach began swelling after breakfast, and I was experiencing severe abdominal pain. Another CT scan showed a partial bowel obstruction. This meant no food or water until my bowel relaxed, but instead of relaxing, my stomach just continued to swell. I awoke at 2:30am on Saturday morning in extreme pain and shortness of breath.

The nurses thought it would be best to insert something called an "NG tube" to vacuum out my stomach and relieve the pain. At the time, I had no idea what an NG tube was—nor had I any idea how painful it would be to insert. The tube was supposed to go up my nose, down my esophagus, and into my stomach. As the nurse was attempting to insert the tube up my nose, she realized that I had a deviated septum, which resulted in the worst bloody nose I have ever experienced. And I cried like a baby.

Unfortunately, they couldn't numb the area because I needed to be able to swallow to help guide the tube down. One of the nurses left to get a pediatric-sized tube and Natalie, the remaining nurse technician, prayed over me. Thankfully, they were able to insert the pediatric-sized tube. It was extremely painful, but somehow God made it bearable. That night, I lay in bed with a tube coming out of my nose to vacuum out my stomach and a tube coming out of my abdomen to drain the pocket of fluid.

The following morning was Taylor's baby shower, and I was devastated that I couldn't be there. Taylor asked if I would FaceTime her at the beginning of the shower to welcome the guests. I wanted so desperately to support Taylor on this special day, so I agreed to FaceTime, but it was a difficult call. I had a tube coming out of my nose, I was bald (but wore a UVA Darden hat just for her), and I felt terrible.

Later that afternoon, I FaceTimed Taylor again to watch her open gifts; I wanted to see the look on her face when she opened the baby afghan that I had crocheted during my chemo treatments at the infusion center. Once the shower was over, I felt like a burden had been lifted from me. I had been so stressed out because I wasn't able to be there in person for this special event, but now I was able to focus on getting well. That afternoon, Dr. E. removed the drain from my abdomen.

I began praying, asking God, "Why this?" and "Why now?" From the very beginning He had assured me that He was in control of this cancer and that I shouldn't worry. But I felt blindsided by this major setback. Within four days of hearing that I was cancer-free, I was back in the hospital with pain far worse than I had experienced during chemo or radiation. It was in this valley of unexpected pain and frustration where I met God again.

He is ever-faithful to reveal Himself to me. I had been praying for God to help my marriage and to help me find new ways to fall in love with Greg again. The Spirit revealed to me how the Lord had been softening Greg's heart, making him tender and caring, and I realized that I was falling in love with him in a whole new way. Twenty plus years of marriage can bring about many challenges in all types of situations, but this was our greatest challenge by far, and God was there for us. I thanked the Lord for showing me how Greg loved me. I thanked the Lord for showing me how Greg lived out his love for me during this time of pain and suffering. I thanked the Lord for showing up in the valley when I needed Him the most.

On Sunday, the nurses removed my NG tube, and I was permitted to eat solids again. I was released from the hospital on Monday and returned home to recover—or rather, *attempt* to recover. Eight days later I was still running a low-grade fever. When I tried to go for a walk, I could only make it down the driveway and back. The next day I tried walking through my neighborhood, but I spent a half hour just walking up the street. I could hardly eat, nothing tasted good, and my weight dropped to 129 pounds.

On Monday, May 16, I called Dr. E. to report that I still had a fever and the area surrounding the cyst was swelling up (yet again) and had turned red. The results of another CT scan indicated that I needed to return to the hospital. I broke down in tears.

And so, round two in the hospital began on Wednesday night. Another drain was put in my abdomen and a PICC line was put back in to administer antibiotics intravenously. Apparently, when the drain was last removed, fluid filled the cyst again, and once more it became infected. The prescription antibiotics I had been taking at home couldn't combat the infection.

I stayed in the hospital for five days and saw significant improvement. I was finally able to walk again and could do laps around the hospital on the second day. When I was released, the doctors left both my drain and PICC line inserted, and I received home health care for the following two to three weeks. A nurse came by periodically to change my PICC line dressing and to check the dressing on my abdomen drain. Slowly but surely, I was recovering.

Even so, I had to cancel yet another trip. Greg and I had planned to meet his son, Sean, in Michigan so that Greg's dad could meet his new great granddaughter, Cora Layne. Even though I couldn't travel, Greg was still able to go. We made arrangements for my younger brother, John, and his daughter, Brooke, to come stay with me. We were able to spend a fun Memorial Day weekend out on the lake together.

Due to my hospital stay, I also had to cancel a surprise trip to the mountains that I had planned for Greg's birthday. It made me sad, realizing how abnormal my life was becoming. It was hard for me to adjust to my new "normal." What is normal? My health will never be the same; I am scarred from being cut open and bald with no eyelashes or eyebrows; I have numb feet from neuropathy; I'm fatigued from operations and treatments, so much so that I can no longer even fathom what I used to do for exercise; and my mind is mush—true chemo brain. Greg has to repeat things to me several times, which tries his patience. But I have to adjust and continue to find joy each day that God has given me to be here.

In early June, I was able to make a much needed and anticipated trip to Chicago with Greg to visit Nikki. I wasn't sure how I would do this since I still had the drain in my stomach, but I was determined. Dr. E. wrote a note to TSA describing all the antibiotics and syringes full of heparin and saline that I would be carrying on. I bought several maxi skirts to hide my huge drain, which hung down to my knees, and off we went. I was so thankful for this wonderful trip and a sense of normalcy.

In mid-June, the drain was removed for good. The infection had cleared and I was regaining my health and strength. I began doing yoga and walking five miles again. Once the drain fully healed, I was able to go in the water. One of my neighbors had a spa day to celebrate; the neighborhood ladies gathered at her hot tub with hors d'oeuvres and wine, and we spent the afternoon relaxing and celebrating. Now that my drain was removed, I also tried paddle boarding, I swam in the lake, and I kayaked! I was so grateful for these little blessings.

But during this time of recovery, my greatest prayer request was that I would be well and strong enough to go to New York in early July for the birth of Baby Bubs to help take care of him and Taylor.

## Day 322 – July 5, 2016

God answered this huge prayer and off to New York I went for Baby Bubs' birth. I flew up on his due date, July 5, and we had a few days of fun along with some craziness as Taylor and Brad moved into a new apartment before the baby decided to make his appearance.

The Sunday following her due date, Taylor wasn't feeling well. She and Brad had planned to meet me at their church that evening, but Brad called and said they thought Taylor might be going into labor. He encouraged me to go to church so that I could meet some of the people who had been praying for me, but only ten minutes into the service, I received another call from Brad, saying that Taylor had started bleeding and they were on their way to the hospital.

I rushed out of church, hailed a cab, and arrived at the hospital in ten minutes. By God's grace, I immediately found Brad, who looked distressed as he sat on a bench in the hallway of the delivery floor. Taylor had been rushed into surgery before he could even kiss her. She needed an emergency C-section because her placenta had detached, and they needed to get the baby out immediately. Within ten minutes, the doctor opened the door for Brad to have a glimpse of his son before he was rushed to the ICU because he had aspirated meconium.

Baby Bubs was christened Henry Luke, and both Brad and Taylor stayed in the hospital for five days while baby Henry recovered in the ICU. I stayed in New York during this time, visiting them in the hospital, running errands for them, and continuing to exercise. One morning, I walked five miles in the park and almost passed out due to a bout of lightheadedness. I ended up walking to the hospital where I did, in fact, proceed to faint. A nurse checked me over while I told her about two other fainting spells I had experienced before coming to New York. The nurses were upset with me because I hadn't told my doctor about it, but I promised I'd call my doctor as soon as I returned to Seneca.

When I returned home, I had a three-month follow-up CT scan to check for tumors. I also called my family doctor, who was concerned about my fainting spells and worried I might have a blood clot. And so ensued a series of tests. When my doctor pulled up my electronic records to go over the test results (for the record, there was nothing wrong from a blood clot standpoint), she happened to see the report of my recent CT scan. After briefly looking it over, she said that it showed a tumor on my liver.

I firmly believe that there are no coincidences in life. I believe that the Lord meant for me to hear this news a week prior to my meeting with Dr. E. in order to have time to process and digest it. This news was certainly a blow, but thankfully, Greg and I were able to get our heads around it. Sure enough, Dr. E. confirmed the tumor, but he was excited that it wasn't located in the treated area of my body—meaning the radiation treatment had been effective. He referred me to a thoracic oncology surgeon who specializes in the liver area, and I scheduled an appointment to meet with him the following week.

As it turns out, I had never been cancer-free. In the meeting with the thoracic oncologist, he showed my most recent CT scan side-by-side with the scan from three months prior, which actually showed a very small tumor—so small it had gone undetected. He believed it was likely a rogue cancer cell that escaped from my pelvic area prior to radiation, attached itself to my liver, and grew rapidly once I had finished my chemo treatments. The good news? It wasn't liver cancer. It was still carcinosarcoma cancer, just in a different part of my body. My doctors were of the opinion that the radiation treatment may have killed the cancer, but there may be a few rogue cancer cells that could grow into tumors that would need to be removed. All things considered, I had so much to be thankful for.

An excerpt from my devotional by Oswald Chambers: "Our real test is in truly believing that God knows what He desires. The things that happen do not happen by chance—they happen entirely by the decree of God. God is sovereignly working out His own purposes. If we are in fellowship and oneness with God and recognize that He is taking us into His purposes, then we will no longer strive to find out what His purposes are…the compelling purpose of God lies behind everything in life, and that God is divinely shaping us into oneness with that purpose" (Chambers, August 5). I knew then (just as I know now) that I can rest in the Lord's peace, believing and trusting in His purpose and His plan.

# Day 343 – July 26, 2016

Surgery to remove the tumor on my liver was scheduled for August 25. The surgeon was confident that he could remove the tumor and get good margins. However, he would have to deflate my lung during the surgery, making for a more difficult recovery. There was a small window of opportunity prior to my surgery to visit Taylor, Brad, and baby Henry in New York. Henry was three weeks old now and Greg had yet to meet him.

In my Jesus Calling devotional I read: "Accept each day just as it comes to you. Do not waste your time and energy wishing for a different set of circumstances" (Young, p.240). The Lord is faithful to encourage me when I spend time with Him. If this cancer has taught me one thing, it's to accept each day as it comes and to make the most of each day.

Prior to going to New York, one of my nurses suggested that I try to see a specialist at Sloan Kettering to get a second opinion on my cancer, especially since Sloan Kettering had seen more cases of carcinosarcoma cancer than Greenville. In order to schedule an appointment, the hospital requires you to send all of your medical records. This was no easy task because I had extensive records at both UNC and Greenville. I had a frenzied week of phone calls and requests to send my records so that we could get an appointment scheduled for that Friday.

On the way to New York, we had a major delay in the Atlanta airport, which was all part of God's grace and perfect timing. Sloan Kettering needed one more piece of information before they could schedule the appointment. I would have missed this call if we hadn't been delayed in Atlanta. Thanks to an amazing nurse at UNC, I was able to get the information sent. It delayed our appointment until the following Monday, but Greg and I extended our trip to accommodate the appointment, and I think it was worthwhile.

At Sloan Kettering, I met with a gynecological oncologist surgeon. He reviewed my records and shared some good news: my doctors in Greenville and Seneca had done everything he would have done. They had left no stone unturned. But there was also some bad news: there wasn't much else to do.

The doctor said that my cancer was acting a bit more like a carcinoma than a sarcoma, and he wanted to present my case to a group of specialists who were convening later that week. After the specialists' meeting, the surgeon called me with the results: the group agreed that I should get a PET scan to look for cellular cancer hotspots. Some members of the group suggested I try chemo first to see if the tumor would shrink (a great way to find out if a certain chemo works; but those who opposed this strategy said that their experience indicates this type of cancer doesn't respond well to chemo) and then surgically remove it if chemo didn't kill the tumor. Another part of the group suggested removing the tumor and then possibly following up with post-op chemo. The specialists also agreed and confirmed that the tumor was on my right diaphragm and not my liver.

I shared this information with Dr. E. in Greenville, who was glad that I had gone to Sloan Kettering and agreed I should get a PET scan to possibly reveal more information. Dr. E. recommended surgery as the first line of defense to remove the cancer. If it's a single tumor, surgery gets it one hundred percent. So, if the PET scan came back negative for other cancer hotspots, surgically removing the one tumor was the best option.

Because cancer is a systemic disease, it was likely that tumors would continue to pop up. I might reach a point when either too many tumors are present or they can't be surgically removed due to location, in which case chemo would be my last resort. If chemo is used too early as a follow-up treatment, it may not be effective later on if multiple tumors pop up.

The results of the PET scan showed the tumor on my liver, but it was difficult to discern its exact location as the specialists at Sloan Kettering had thought the tumor was on my right diaphragm. Thankfully, the PET scan didn't show any cancer hotspots. Thus, surgery to remove the tumor was scheduled for August 25.

# God's Confirmation
# of Healing

# Day 373 – August 25, 2016

The surgery lasted two hours, and, as the specialists at Sloan Kettering had predicted, the tumor was in my diaphragm after all. The surgeon had to deflate my lung during the operation, but he was able to get good margins around the tumor. Sewing up my diaphragm was interesting because they couldn't pull the diaphragm together (it doesn't stretch and the capacity needs to stay the same), so they stitched back and forth until the hole was filled with surgical thread, and eventually scar tissue would fill it in completely.

I was only in recovery for about an hour, and I don't remember waking up until I had been back in my hospital room for quite a while. The associate pastor, Tony, from my church paid me a visit, but I was exceedingly groggy from the morphine and could barely talk or breathe. On Saturday morning, I asked the nurses to take me off of the morphine and to pull the epidural so that I could breathe better and start walking to aid in my recovery. By that afternoon, I was walking laps around the hospital.

Greg later told me that as I was going into surgery, he was praying for no more cancer. I'm so thankful that Greg prayed to Jesus on my behalf, but I also wanted Greg to know that God is in control. I prayed for Greg's faith to increase as my pain becomes harder to handle, and that the Lord would continue to be a light shining through me so that others would see Him and His work.

Once home from the hospital, I started my walking routine to strengthen my body. On my walks, I listen to sermons or good Christian music, and it is during these times that I feel closest to the Lord. Oftentimes, I would end my walk at the large cross on the lake, where I would pray and pour my heart out to God, knowing how great He is.

Oswald Chambers said, "God has established things so that prayer, on the basis of redemption, changes the way a person looks at things. Prayer is not a matter of changing things externally, but one of working miracles in a person's inner nature. [...] Believe steadfastly on Him and everything that challenges you will strengthen your faith. There is a continual testing in the life of faith up to the point of our physical death, which is the last great test. Faith is absolute trust in God—trust that could never imagine that He would forsake us" (Chambers, August 28, 29).

## Day 387 – September 8, 2016

September 8, 2016 marked the one-year anniversary of my cancer diagnosis and first surgery. I praised God for carrying me through the past year and for blessing me with a speedy recovery from my most recent surgery. I was finally off of pain medications, and I was walking five to six miles daily. Walking was the only exercise I was allowed to do—no yoga or biking for six weeks so that my diaphragm could heal properly. I was eager to heal quickly because I was itching to get back into yoga. I also wanted to start biking again because Greg and I had just purchased new bicycles.

In the past, God has affirmed my healing by speaking through friends and family members, but I love when He does so through perfect strangers. He is faithful to remind me of His goodness and sovereignty.

I was out walking with a friend one afternoon when two women with a baby stroller came running up to us. One of the women (I later found out her name was Keri) said, "Excuse me, do you mind if I ask you what you are going through? Because God has placed on my heart to speak with you and to tell you that you are healed. I've been prompted many times by His Spirit to stop and tell you this when I have passed you walking. This time, the prompting was so strong, I knew I would be disobedient to the Lord if I didn't stop you and convey His message. Today, God said to tell you. I don't have a clue what you are dealing with and I don't even know you, but God's pressing on my heart is just too strong not to tell you this."

I was blown away. From the very beginning of my cancer journey, I knew that God would heal me, but I was astounded that He should use a complete stranger to encourage me and to deliver this message about my healing. I then shared my cancer story with Keri and the other woman, Lynda. As it turns out, Keri had lost her dad a year ago to esophageal cancer and Lynda's mother had just passed away. They are both strong prayer warriors! I was reminded of the promptings in my past from the Holy Spirit and how important it is to act on them. When you do, you will not only bless others but you will also be blessed in return.

## Day 408 – September 20, 2016

Toward the end of September, I had a six-month follow-up appointment with my radiation oncologist in Greenville. Prior to my appointment, she was looking over my medical records—reading about my infection and latest surgery—and was unsure of what my emotional state would be since she had a feeling (based on my records) that I wasn't cancer-free. What she got though was a big smile and a hug. We spent an hour together while I brought her up to speed on my medical life and then shared how God was continually at work through my journey. I also shared with her how I had been praying and asking God how He will continue to use me when I'm healed from this cancer.

Over the course of the past year, my faith had been strengthened so much and my relationship with Jesus had become deeper; I felt there was something He was preparing me for. My doctor then asked if I would consider speaking at her Bible study. She thought the women could benefit from my story of hope and faith and my powerful living testimony. I was uplifted thinking that this may be the next chapter in my journey—encouraging and helping others who may be questioning their faith while dealing with their individual struggles.

After my last surgery, Dr. E. had sent the tumor off to pathology. As the oncologist at Sloan Kettering had supposed, the results of the pathology indicated carcinoma cells (not carcinosarcoma), similar to ovarian cancer, which increased my chances of being alive in five years from twenty percent to fifty percent—a sweet indicator of my healing process. What's more, it seems that this type of tumor responds well to chemo, whereas carcinosarcoma does not. He scheduled me to return in two weeks for a CT scan, and he set up an appointment with a medical oncologist specialist who works with rare tumors and clinical trials. He also sent my tumor off to look at genetic indicators, which may help identify what clinical trials I might be eligible for.

At that time, I felt so healthy that it was difficult for me to think about my cancer returning. Last April when my CT scan came back clean and I was declared cancer-free, I had begun journaling the epilogue to my story, thinking my journey had come to an end. However, God, in His infinite wisdom, had other plans.

Greg and I met with the medical oncologist specialist to discuss the pathology results, which showed the genetic makeup of my most recent tumor. I knew I had a rare cancer, of course, but I guess I didn't realize just *how rare*. As rare as uterine cancer is, only one to two percent of those diagnosed have carcinosarcoma. What's more, the pathology results showed that my tumor had cancer cells containing HER2 receptors. Mine was the only documented case of uterine cancer cells with a HER2 receptor. These receptors are usually found in breast cancer cells as well as some ovarian and colon cancer cells.

There are FDA-approved drugs on the market for treatment of these cancers with an HER2 receptor, but they're not approved to use on uterine cancer patients. The HER2 receptor is like a keyhole that unlocks the cancer cell, allowing the drug to penetrate and kill it. Treatment has been successful in patients with breast, colon, and ovarian cancers, but because the drug isn't FDA-approved for uterine cancer, my treatment would constitute a clinical trial.

This oncologist advised me to get a PET scan and a heart echo (because a side effect of the treatment drug is that it affects the flow of blood through the heart). If the PET scan came back positive for cancer hotspots, he wanted me to apply to the drug manufacturer, asking them to donate the drug for a trial. If approved, I would undergo six more months of treatment to see if they could kill the cancer. On the other hand, if the PET scan came back negative, I would need to decide whether or not to undergo the treatment. It's quite possible I could still have microscopic cancer cells, but without a tumor we wouldn't be able to discern if the drug was effectively treating the microscopic cells.

I was torn about what to do and how to proceed. If the PET scan came back positive, the choice was clear. But what if it came back negative? Should I opt in or out of treatment? On November 29, I received the results: it was negative. After much prayer and deliberation, I opted not to follow through with the treatment, as we would have no way of knowing if it was effective. However, this meant I was running the risk of allowing microscopic cancer cells—if indeed there were any—to grow uninhibited. Since the scan showed I was clean and I felt so healthy, I once again *felt* healed of this dreadful disease.

## Day 486 –December 16, 2016

After Thanksgiving, Greg and I traveled to Denver to celebrate Cora's first birthday. While there, I received a call from my brother, John, saying that our mother was in the hospital and might not make it. She had just undergone surgery for a blood clot in her leg and was currently recovering in the ICU. I FaceTimed my mom to tell her how much I loved her and that I was coming to see her the next day. I received a second call from John at 4am, saying the doctors were losing her. Her blood pressure had dropped dramatically, but somehow they were able to stabilize her.

Early the next morning, Greg and I changed our return flights from Denver so that once we flew into Atlanta, I could fly to Greensboro to see my mom and Greg could fly home to Seneca. On my flight from Atlanta to Greensboro, I was sitting in first class with an empty seat next to me when the flight attendant directed a young man up to the empty seat. It was divine intervention. As it turns out, the young man was a pastor! I spoke to him about my cancer journey, what was going on with my mother, and how I was concerned I wouldn't make it to the hospital before she passed. The pastor spent the rest of the flight praying over me, both for my cancer and for my mother; what an amazing example of how God works. There are no coincidences in life!

My brother picked me up from the airport and took me straight to the hospital. I arrived in time. My mom opened her eyes and knew that I was there. I told her I wouldn't leave her. I encouraged the rest of my family to go home to rest; I would stay the night and call if anything changed. I spent some time alone with my mother, talking to her. She opened her eyes periodically and appeared to be frightened, but I calmed her and reminded her of where she was and why she couldn't talk (she had a tube down her throat to help her breathe).

The ICU visiting hours ended at 11pm so I retreated to the hospital lobby, where I curled up in a chair, using my purse as a pillow. Just one month prior, I was dealing with cancer surgery, and now here I was dealing with my mother's impending death. My mind raced and I wondered how much I could handle. I felt so overwhelmed. My only comfort was knowing that the Lord never gives us more than we can handle. He gives us abundant grace to accomplish all things through Him who gives us strength.

At 4am, I went back to the ICU to sit with my mom. Within a mere fifteen minutes, the doctors started losing her, and the nurse told me to call my siblings. When there was nothing more they could do, the doctors backed away while I stood by my mother's bed, stroking her hair, telling her how much I loved her and to relax and go into Jesus' arms. After fifteen minutes, she passed peacefully, and I was grateful to be there alone with her. Just then, my family started to arrive.

Death has a way of bringing out the good and the bad in people. Some cope well with grief, holding onto the peace that surpasses all understanding, while others let it fuel a fire of frustration and anguish. Unfortunately, my mother's death brought about family misery, hurt, and tribulation that carried on for months. Through time, God has healed the wounds of division, but I know that our family will never be the same again. I feel blessed knowing that my mom passed away during a "healthy" period in my journey, believing that I was healed from this cancer.

We planned to have the funeral during the week between Christmas and New Year's Eve so as to not disrupt everyone's holiday plans. Despite our circumstances, Greg and I passed a joyful Christmas in New York with Brad,

Taylor, and baby Henry, and we returned in time for my mother's funeral on December 30 in Amherst, Virginia.

# Day 502 – January 1, 2017

I began 2017 feeling as healthy as I had ever been. In keeping with stereotypical New Year's resolutions, I resolved to join a gym. And I did! I took high intensity interval training (HIIT) classes. Prior to my cancer diagnosis, I had taken HIIT classes and was in the best shape of my life. This time around, the classes were more difficult, but I was ready for the challenge. I pushed myself and worked out consistently throughout the month of January, and much to my delight I regained my cardio and muscle strength.

Life began to feel normal again. Now that I thought I was cancer-free, Greg and I felt it was important for our lives to regain a sense of normalcy, so we took a long-overdue trip to Key West, just the two of us. It was the perfect reprieve not only from the cold, but also from the maddening routine of surgeries, cancer treatments, doctor appointments, and blood tests that had taken over our lives.

At the end of February, I traveled to New York for a week to babysit Henry while Brad and Taylor took a trip to France to go skiing. I was so thankful that I was well enough to babysit Henry, and I was honored that my daughter trusted me with her son—enough to leave the country! Taylor had made arrangements to keep their regular nanny, Sabrina, during the weekdays. That way, Henry would stay on schedule and I would have a chance to rest during the day. In the evenings, I had Henry all to myself for dinner, bath, and bedtime. He was an angel!

On the weekend when Sabrina wasn't there, Rhonda, my sister-in-law, came up to the city to help with the daily activities and spend quality time with Henry. It was a delightful time for the three of us.

Prior to going to New York, I had my three-month follow-up CT scan. I received the results right before I left. The good news? No tumors. The bad news? A suspicious lymph node. Dr. E. then sent me off for a PET scan to get a better look at the lymph node, and I received the results of the PET scan while I was in New York.

It was Friday, Henry was napping, and Sabrina and I were in the kitchen when I received the call from Dr. E. The tumor in my lymph node had grown and was hot with cancer. To make matters worse, there was another hotspot between my heart and right lung. I scheduled an appointment with a lung oncologist for the day after I returned to Seneca.

After these phone calls, Sabrina started crying. She told me that she knew God had placed her there to hear my bad news. She shared with me that she had recently received a report from her doctor indicating that she had some pre-cancerous cells. The report scared her so badly that she never followed up with her doctor. After seeing what I had gone through and continued to experience, she felt God lay it on her heart to call her doctor immediately and see what tests she needed to have done to take care of her concerns. Today, thankfully, everything is fine with her, and I continue to thank God for how he uses my cancer to touch others.

# Darkness Closes In

## Day 562 – March 2, 2017

Greg and I met with the lung oncologist, who pulled up the scan showing the hotspot between my heart and right lung. He could remove it, but he wasn't sure if it was in my lung or in a fatty layer in a crevice outside my heart. He wouldn't know until he got in. He hoped to do the surgery robotically but warned me that there could be issues. He might even need to break my breast bone to remove the spot. To add to the uncertainty, the doctors and radiation technologists were uncertain as to whether the hotspot was actually a cancer tumor or an area of collapsed air sacs in the lung. Surgery was the only way to find out.

Surgery was scheduled to remove both tumors—the lymph node that was hot with cancer and the spot supposedly between my lung and heart—for the next Friday, March 10. The week prior to the surgery, I had a pulmonary test and pre-op. It was a frustrating week because I kept receiving mixed messages about when and where to show up for surgery. By Thursday night, I was thoroughly frustrated and anxious. My friend, Keri, prayed over me; she not only prayed for a successful surgery but also that I would be a light in the hospital. On Friday morning during the drive to Greenville, Taylor and Brad called and prayed over me. They prayed for peace, calmness, and for the cancer to be gone.

I arrived at the hospital and went straight to pre-op. One of the nurses tried three times to start an IV, but she couldn't find a vein and had to get another nurse. This simply added to my frustration and anxiety. As previously discussed with my oncologist surgeon, the operation was going to be a CT-guided procedure. This meant that I would have yet another CT scan, and the technicians would insert a wire with ink to locate the spot so that it would be identifiable during surgery when they collapsed my lung.

After the scan was complete, the technicians left the room to review the films. I was left alone in the claustrophobic scanner, so I closed my eyes and began thanking Jesus for where I was and that He would never leave nor forsake me. After what seemed an eternity, the technicians and doctor returned. They couldn't believe what they were seeing on the scan: the spot between my heart and right lung had shrunk to practically nothing and they decided to cancel the operation altogether.

I was overwhelmed with emotion and began crying. One of the nurses teared up and began praising God and shouting Hallelujah. Everyone was in awe of what they had witnessed. It's an extreme rarity to receive good news about cancer! I was wheeled back to pre-op where Greg and the other nurses had already heard the good news, and they gathered around me, elated. I still had to undergo the second scheduled operation for the lymph node, but it only took twenty minutes. I was in post-op for about forty-five minutes and then I was sent home.

What began as a stressful day filled with anxiety about surgery near my heart ended as a short day in the hospital with a minor surgery. As Keri had prayed, the Lord again used me as a light and many were touched by my faith in Jesus that day at the hospital. I am so thankful to the Lord that He is in control and that He knows each moment of each day I live and breathe. I am thankful that He uses me as a witness for Him.

Unfortunately, cancer is smart. Once you're on a chemo, the cancer teaches itself to mutate in order to survive the treatment, thereby rendering the chemo treatment ineffective for future use. This is why, in many cases, a patient can't receive the same chemo treatment twice. However, my nurse advocate told me about another patient of hers who also had carcinosarcoma cancer. This patient underwent a hysterectomy and was cancer-free for three years. When the cancer returned after three years, she was able to take the same chemo again because her body had returned to its pre-chemo state, and the cancer didn't recognize that the chemo had been used in the past. This gave me hope to possibly use Carboplatin/Taxol again, especially since my doctors kept talking about using Ifosfamide, one of the most difficult chemos on your body, as my next treatment.

The tumor that was removed from my lymph node had been sent off to pathology, and shortly thereafter, Dr. E. called with the results. As it turns out, the tumor contained carcinosarcoma cancer cells (like my original cancer), not sarcoma cancer cells (like the doctors had speculated). My tumor was also sent off for genetic modeling, and I scheduled a follow-up appointment three weeks out (when the results came back) to discuss my post-operative treatment options.

The results of the genetic modeling showed that my tumor had a receptor called FGF2. In light of this information, there were four treatment options available to me. The first option was a clinical trial in the form of an oral medication that penetrates the FGF2 receptor and hopefully kills the cancer. Thankfully, the only major side effect of this drug was diarrhea. The second option was to try immunotherapy. The side effect of immunotherapy was developing an autoimmune disease, but managing an autoimmune disease is much easier than managing cancer. In fact, many patients who take immunotherapy experience few to no side effects.

The third option was to try the original chemo I had again to see if there were any results. Finally, the fourth option was to do nothing and simply wait to see if another tumor developed. For the two clinical trials (options one and two) I needed an active cancer tumor that the doctors could measure in order to qualify for the trials. This enables the doctors to measure the effectiveness of the trial drug against the size of the tumor, assessing its growth rate and whether or not it shrinks or dies.

With the knowledge we had at that time, Greg and I chose to do nothing and wait. I had a CT scan scheduled for May 10 to see if there was any change. Greg and I would make a treatment decision pending the outcome of that scan. Dr. E. scheduled an appointment for me with the medical oncologist specialist to hear more about the recent clinical trials for FGF2. That way, I could be ready to make a decision when the time came. I was so anxious about possibly having to undergo chemo again. I cried out to God about my anxiety and He heard me.

# Day 602 – April 11, 2017

During my meeting with the medical oncologist specialist, he informed me that the trial for the new drug targeting the FGF2 receptor was closed, but another one might open in the future. However, the immunotherapy trial was still open. Greg and I stressed our concerns about the side effects of immunotherapy and, more importantly, the possibility of developing an autoimmune disease. The doctor laughed off our concerns—as only a cancer research doctor would do—and said that he could manage any autoimmune disease with steroids. His job was to kill the cancer.

The doctor again recommended that I get a CT scan in the next week (instead of waiting until May 10) so that he could put me in the immunotherapy trial if a tumor showed up. I felt like things were moving far too quickly. At that time, I actually felt quite healthy; I was taking HIIT classes and regaining my strength. When I'm in a "healthy state," it's difficult for me to think about my cancer. I want to focus on my health instead.

In that moment, talking with the doctor, I felt like my whole life revolved around doctor appointments, surgeries, cancer treatments, and blood tests. What I wanted most was to call a timeout. And so I did. I politely declined his approach to bump up the scan and told him that I would proceed with getting the scan as originally planned on May 10, which was only a month away.

In the weeks leading up to May 10, I was irritable, depressed, and anxious about the possibility of more treatments. So many cancer patients have surgery followed by post-op treatments, and then they are declared cancer-free. Even though I had heard the words "cancer-free" early on, I have never actually been free of cancer. Instead, I was left with an empty space, a little hollow that those words should have filled. To make matters worse, I hadn't felt the Lord's presence lately. Construction at the house (landscaping, stone work, house painting, etc.) had caused me to miss my morning quiet time by the fireplace on the back porch. Since moving to Seneca, that spot has always been my "happy place" to meet with Jesus.

When I was finally able to return to Him, I immediately saw a difference in my attitude (not surprisingly!). The more we seek God, the more He shows up and the more we feel His presence. Ultimately, it's an act of obedience. We have the choice not to seek Him, but when we faithfully and obediently seek Him, we are rewarded with His presence, a true and great reward.

In the wake of my depression, I decided to spend a few weeks *not* thinking about my cancer. And so, toward the end of April, I went to Sarasota, Florida to babysit Henry while Brad and Taylor attended the wedding of a close friend. Henry and I had a wonderful time playing on the beach, floating in the swimming pool, and soaking up the sunshine.

It was a joy to watch Henry experience things for the first time. Growing up in a concrete jungle had precluded him from experiencing things like feeling grass and sand under his bare feet. For Henry, to walk barefoot outside was to experience a whole new world. As I held him by the hands to walk him on the grass, he would lift one foot—almost as if he were doing a Tai Chi or yoga pose—and just stand there, not wanting to put his foot back down.

At the end of the trip, Taylor flew out of Sarasota for business, and I flew back to New York with Brad and Henry to help out for two days until Taylor returned. Poor little Henry had a fever and a cold, and I ended up catching it from him. It was the first cold I had contracted while having cancer, which I took to mean that my immune system was fairly intact!

Despite those four to five weeks of *not* thinking about my cancer, my depression seemed to be getting worse. By the first week of May, I was crying every day. My family doctor suggested a counselor and a mild medication. Mother's Day and my mother's 90th birthday (if she were still alive) had come and gone. Since my mother's death in December, I hadn't had time to properly grieve. To make matters worse, my sister hadn't spoken to me for three months, and I think that losing her friendship likely contributed to my depression.

When I had my CT scan on May 10, I told the nurse that if I received bad news, I would likely go off the deep end. Cancer is such a lonely disease because no one (aside from other cancer patients) really knows what you're going through. To help remedy my loneliness and depression, I signed up to volunteer in a new woman-to-woman mentoring program at the hospital. The program pairs patients who have the same cancer diagnosis; one is the mentor and the other is the mentee. I decided to volunteer as a mentor because I felt like I could offer another patient encouragement and support. I filled out the application documents, took the online training courses, underwent two TB tests, completed the enrollment process, and then waited…and waited.

I had felt like perhaps this was God's calling because it was something I could do to give back, but I never received a response. The hospital couldn't pair anyone with me because my cancer was so rare. My cancer was so rare that I couldn't even find a cancer support group for myself. I felt so completely alone.

At last, I began taking a mild medication and scheduled to meet with a Christian counselor at the end of

May. Within a week of taking medication I began feeling better—not quite my old self, but on the way.

# Day 638 – May 17, 2017

On May 17, I met with Dr. E. to discuss the results of my CT scan. We spent the first few minutes discussing my depression, and then he broke the news to me: my scan showed another tumor. I cried when I heard the news. I was thankful I had been on medication because I felt like I just couldn't handle any more bad news. I knew that God hadn't forsaken me, but the constant bad news was wearing me down, and it was wearing Greg down, too. Again, I started to feel like Job in the Bible.

The tumor, which was about the size of a quarter, was located on my right adrenal gland above my kidney. It was in a tricky place to operate because it was so close to my vena cava, and the surgeon would have to remove a lot of organs to reach it. Instead of operating, Dr. E. suggested I meet with the oncology specialist again to discuss getting in a clinical trial. I drove to Spartanburg to meet with him, and we reviewed the clinical trials available. We also scheduled a biopsy of the tumor and a PET scan (to identify possible cancer hotspots) for the next week.

Before my next meeting, I walked with my friend, Keri. She had felt a pressing from the Lord that I needed to talk. We walked and talked for over two hours. Keri prayed over me before we parted ways, and I immediately felt like a heaviness was lifted from me. I praise God for Keri's friendship; He is faithful to bring the right people into your life when you need them. In one of my deepest valleys, God gave me Keri. Once that heaviness had been lifted from me, I felt like I had more mental clarity to review the clinical trials and make a decision.

In my follow-up meeting with the oncologist specialist, I told him that Greg and I had decided on the trial that targets the FGF2 receptor (not the immunotherapy trial), and he gave me a copy of the protocol to take home and review. Before leaving Greenville, I stopped in to see my radiation oncologist. It was a relief to be with her as I cried and told her what was going on both medically and emotionally. Somewhat to my surprise, she asked me to speak at her Bible study class in ten days. I was thrilled with the idea and my spirits were lifted.

You may remember that she had asked me some time ago (when I was in much better health) if I would consider speaking to her class. I had readily agreed, but, as she later shared with me, the class only consisted of a small handful of people at that time. She didn't want me to come speak to such a small group, and so she had opted to wait until the class had been built back up with a good number of consistent members.

For me, the difference was that I no longer felt healthy. I had a tumor; I was completely unsure of what my future entailed; and I was in emotional turmoil. And yet, I felt like there was no better time to speak to a group of women. I know that each of us is broken and suffering in some way. I just so happen to be suffering from a rare cancer.

That same day, I had my first appointment with a pastoral counselor. I gave her a broad overview of what was going on, and it felt good not only to talk to someone about my cancer, but also to have a Christian woman help me deal with my emotions. My counselor prayed over me after my appointment and I was so grateful. Just like Keri had been sent to me at the right time, so the Lord sent this counselor to me at just the right time.

The following day, I went to Greenville for my biopsy on the tumor above my right kidney. Greg and I were told to wait in the holding room. For some entirely inexplicable reason, Greg expressed that he felt like doing a ballet dance...although he knows absolutely nothing about ballet. And so, my husband began doing ballet leaps across the room! We both started laughing so hard that the nurses came rushing in, thinking that I was having a major crying fit about my cancer and impending biopsy. When they found out what was going on, they too broke out laughing.

The episode provided some comedic relief and was a pleasant precursor to my biopsy, which went well. Instead of being put under, I laid on my side while they guided the needle in because they needed me to keep breathing in order to prevent my lung from collapsing. The sad news was that I couldn't use our new hot tub for a week because the doctor wanted to ensure that the spot completely healed over first.

The day after my biopsy, I had a PET scan to check for any cancer hotspots. Then, I scheduled a follow-up appointment with my specialist for the next week so that we could discuss the results of both the biopsy and PET scan.

I had been participating in an acupuncture clinical trial for the neuropathy in my feet that I had developed from the chemo treatments. I was nearing the end of my 12-week trial and for this I was quite thankful. The trial was offered by the hospital, but it was conducted at an oriental medicine facility. In addition to performing the acupuncture treatments, the doctor at the facility had gotten into the habit of pestering me with questions about my cancer and offering his suggestions for nutrition and healing. On several occasions he mentioned ozone therapy, which apparently isn't approved in the U.S. (many people go to Germany for it), but somehow he was able to offer the treatment.

The premise behind ozone therapy is that it increases the oxygen in your blood to better enable healing. I discussed the therapy with Greg, but we both agreed that I was in great hands with Dr. E. If all else fails, perhaps we would consider ozone therapy as a last resort. We have been amused at the advice we've received from people, knowing that they all mean well. But we put this one in the same category as "if I only ate organic tomatoes, I would be cured!"

To my dismay, the acupuncture doctor seemed indignant that I declined his offer to try the therapy. When he found out that I was planning to start a clinical trial, he told me that doctors would treat me like a specimen, that they were only using me to help them find a cure for cancer, and that they weren't focused on actually curing me. He further claimed that I would be poked and prodded to death, and when I died my doctors would simply find a new guinea pig. Needless to say, this was the *last* thing I needed to hear. I was already dealing with a host of issues that had culminated in depression—and I certainly didn't need this doctor adding to those issues!

I think that depression can be more debilitating to a believer than a non-believer. "If then the light within you is darkness, how great is that darkness!" (*NIV*, Matt. 6:23). As believers, we are children of light. So, when darkness invades our hearts and minds through depression…how great is that darkness! However, I continued to praise God and believe in His sovereignty and His hand in my healing process.

# Day 654 – June 2, 2017

At the beginning of June, Sean and Cora came to visit for four days. Greg and Sean enjoyed father-and-son time assembling our new outdoor sauna while I thoroughly enjoyed spending time with my granddaughter, Cora. It was a delight to have her all to myself, and I feel like we truly bonded.

Prior to my next appointment with the specialist, I read the protocol for the clinical trial. My biggest concern was that this trial was in "dose escalation phase 1," the phase where they continue to escalate the dose until finding the right amount that kills the cancer while inducing the fewest side effects. My concern was that I didn't have enough time on my side for them to figure out the right dose.

Greg and I prayed for clear direction at my appointment with the specialist, and the Lord was faithful to answer our prayers—just not in the way we had expected. First, the good news: the clinical trial was no longer in the escalation phase. The trial was in "phase 1 expansion," meaning the doctors had determined the best dose to hopefully kill the cancer while inducing the fewest side effects. This made me feel much more assured about beginning the trial, especially because it likely wouldn't be open later, whereas other trials would be.

Next, the bad news. According to my PET scan, the tumor had quadrupled in size and I had three more tumors: one in my lymph system (in the center of my body) and two in my liver. My eyes welled up with tears while the doctor told me that my cancer had metastasized and was growing rapidly. This wasn't the news I had expected to hear. I knew then as I know now that all things happen in God's perfect timing, but I was so hoping the time had come for me to be healed.

We read and signed the consent forms for the trial and left. When we returned home, we shared the news with Sean and Cora that my cancer had metastasized; it was a somber moment. They left shortly afterward to catch their flight home to Denver. It wasn't the most pleasant way for them to end their vacation!

On Thursday I went to the hospital for a CT scan in preparation for the trial. I was getting on a first-name basis with the CT nurses…not a good thing! After the scan, I stopped at the Cancer Center to update my chemo nurse, April, on my condition. During my chemo treatments, April had become a dear friend to me. We both teared up as I shared the latest news with her.

The Lord is ever-faithful to meet me in my valleys, and this time He met me through April. She shared a song with me: "Even If"[1] by Mercy Me.

"They say sometimes you win some
Sometimes you lose some
And right now, right now I'm losing bad
I've stood on this stage night after night
Reminding the broken it'll be alright
But right now, oh right now I just can't

It's easy to sing
When there's nothing to bring me down
But what will I say
When I'm held to the flame
Like I am right now

---

[1] MercyMe. "Even If." *Lifer*, 2017, track 5. *Genius*, https://genius.com/Mercyme-even-if-lyrics.

I know You're able and I know You can
Save through the fire with Your mighty hand
But even if You don't
My hope is You alone

They say it only takes a little faith
To move a mountain
Well, good thing
A little faith is all I have, right now
But God, when You choose to leave mountains unmovable
Oh give me the strength to be able to sing
It is well with my soul

You've been faithful, You've been good
All of my days
Jesus, I will cling to you
Come what may
Cause I know You're able
I know You can

I know the sorrow, and I know the hurt
Would all go away, if You'd just say the word
But even if You don't
My hope is You alone

It is well with my soul
It is well, it is well with my soul"

April said that she thinks of me and sheds a tear every time she hears this song. My favorite lines in the song are about knowing the Lord is able to heal me, but even if He doesn't, my hope is in Him alone! She went on to tell me that I was the most positive person she had met, and she knows that my positivity is Jesus' light in me. I was so encouraged and uplifted by April's words during this sad time.

## Day 663 – June 11, 2017

For the past week, I had been preparing to share my story with my radiation oncologist's Bible study class. Before the class, I gave her an update on my cancer and how it had metastasized. I wasn't sure if she still wanted me to come since I wasn't in my best frame of mind. However, she felt it was God's perfect timing and that He would use me to speak to the women in her class.

In preparation, I read through my journal for the first time. It was difficult (even for me!) to believe what I had been through over the course of the past two years. I prayed that God would give me the right words to say and that my story would touch each woman. I took ten pages of notes, but when I spoke I only read the first and last pages, letting God fill in the middle. I spoke for two hours, and when I had finished there was not a dry eye in the room.

My doctor then read a scripture from Luke that the Lord had laid on her heart, "And a woman was there who had been subject to bleeding for twelve years, but no one could heal her. She came up behind him and touched the edge of his cloak, and immediately her bleeding stopped. 'Who touched me?' Jesus asked. When they all denied it, Peter said, 'Master, the people are crowding and pressing against you.' But Jesus said, 'Someone touched me; I know that power has gone out from me.' Then the woman, seeing that she could not go unnoticed, came trembling and fell at his feet. In the presence of all the people, she told why she had touched him and how she had been instantly healed. Then he said to her, 'Daughter, your faith has healed you. Go in peace'" (*NIV*, Luke 8:43-48).

This woman waited twelve years to be healed and no doctor could heal her. But she *knew* that if she just touched Jesus' robe she would be healed. What great faith!

Upon hearing this scripture read aloud, the Lord reminded me that He had used that scripture before in my healing process, from my daughter-in-law's friend in Denver. The Lord had placed that scripture on her heart about me. Just as in the Bible, it's important when God repeats things.

My doctor, who is also my sweet friend, then asked some of the men from the men's Bible study to stay after their meeting so that they could all anoint me with oil, lay hands on me, and pray over me. It was an incredible experience to hear fifteen people praying over me at the same time (reminding me of the sweet prayer time I experienced during my travels in Kenya). After ten minutes of praying and claiming my healing in Jesus' name, they slowly removed their hands, and I felt something like an electrical surge run through my body. It was like nothing I had ever felt before.

It was an amazing night of sharing and witnessing God's healing power. After this experience, I felt even more encouraged to write my story, in the hope that others could benefit from God's grace and mercy in my life. Although it's difficult for me to share my story, it's still a gift for me to testify about my faith to others, encouraging them in their walks with Christ. God is sovereign over everything, and it's my prayer that He will continue to use my story to encourage others.

On Monday, I spent the day in Greenville completing the required tests (a blood test, an EKG, and an eye exam, to name a few) for the clinical trial. I also met with my doctor's assistant, who was extremely knowledgeable and gave me detailed information about the trial. With her wealth of knowledge and information, she seemed like the perfect person to ask about my prognosis. I knew full well that God was in control, but I also wanted to understand my timeframe from an earthly perspective, especially if the clinical trial didn't work.

The assistant told me, quite frankly, that I probably had six to eight months to live if the trial drugs were ineffective. This hit me like a ton of bricks, and I couldn't help but tear up. But I thanked her for being up front with me.

While I was overwhelmed by the morbidity of my prognosis, I also knew that God never changes; He is the same yesterday, today, and forever. He performed miracles in Biblical times and continues to do so today. I also knew that He has the power to heal me, and I chose to continue trusting in His perfect timing.

I shared this information with Taylor and Greg. Taylor was glad to have a doctor's realistic medical opinion. We didn't want to dwell on it, of course, but it was an important timeline to work within. I tucked it aside as my earthly knowledge but continued to focus on the Lord and the great things He had done and continued to do.

## Day 666 – June 14, 2017

Wednesday, June 14 marked the beginning of the clinical trial. I went to Greenville where I picked up the solid pills from the pharmacy, took the first dose, and waited two hours to have another EKG. When the EKG showed that the dose hadn't affected my heart (a good precaution), I was sent home.

Cue the side effects. I had been told that diarrhea was a major side effect of the pills, but I certainly wasn't prepared for it to set in immediately—right after dinner I had a major bout of diarrhea. I could only hope and pray it wouldn't happen every day!

The following day, I received a call from one of Taylor's friends in New York. She has a prayer room and prays over people for healing. She had felt the Holy Spirit pressing on her heart to pray over me, and she did so over the phone. Afterward, I felt a rush through my body, similar to what I had experienced when I received prayer at my doctor's Bible study. Taylor's friend told me that she had seen that happen to other people as well and feels that it's the power of the Holy Spirit.

In mid-June, my brother, John, and his family came to visit for the weekend. As I shared my prognosis with them we all shed tears. I'm so thankful that I can lean on them through this journey! We enjoyed a beautiful family weekend on the lake, boating, kayaking, and paddle boarding. We also went in the hot tub and tried out the sauna. After their departure, I felt the Holy Spirit laying two scriptures on my heart: "Let us hold unswervingly to the hope we profess, for he who promised is faithful" (*NIV*, Heb. 10:23), and "'For I know the plans I have for you,' declares the Lord, 'plans to prosper you and not to harm you, plans to give you hope and a future'" (*NIV*, Jer. 29:11).

Two weeks had passed since my last meeting with my counselor, and I had quite a bit to share with her, especially about answered prayer. We had prayed for clear direction regarding the clinical trial and, even though we received an answer we weren't expecting, the Lord had made the direction clear. My counselor, who is an active pastor in a church, expressed amazement at how God was working in my life, and she even wondered if my visits to her were helping me. She told me how much my visits were helping her and strengthening her faith. I was surprised that a pastor would be amazed at my strength throughout this cancer journey. Doesn't she know it's the power of Christ in me?

On a regular basis, I'm confronted with people telling me how "amazing" I am. Always, my response is that it's not me but Christ in me who gives me the strength to endure. I'm grateful that the Lord has used my cancer and my story to open the eyes of non-believers as well as believers.

On June 22, I went to my oncology specialist's office to have my blood work reviewed. While there, I ran into Dr. E.'s nurse, Hillary. I asked if and when I would see her again, since I had effectively been "turned over" to the oncology specialist for the clinical trial. Hillary said that once the trial medicine stops the cancer growth, they would take me back on as a patient and continue overseeing my cancer.

Over the course of the past two years, I had seen countless doctors, but Hillary and Dr. E. had been the singular constant in my life, overseeing my cancer treatments and walking with me through this journey. Sometimes I feel like I'm playing musical chairs with doctors, constantly moving from one to another. It was such a relief to know that they would still be there for me and continue to oversee the process.

# Day 677 – June 25, 2017

At the end of June, I traveled to New York to visit Taylor, Brad, and Henry. Taylor and I were both upset that we hadn't seen each other since receiving the news that my cancer had metastasized. Henry's first birthday was only two weeks away, but I couldn't wait until then. I was eager to spend quality time with Taylor and Henry, and I knew it would be more difficult to squeeze in some quality time during his busy birthday weekend. So off I went to New York!

It was a very short and tiring trip. When I arrived on Sunday evening, Taylor and Henry were waiting for me on the sidewalk so I could give him a hug before he went to bed. Taylor and I sat up talking, but we didn't stay up late since we were both tired.

I spent Monday with Sabrina (the nanny) and Henry while Taylor worked from home and while Brad went to work to hand in his official resignation. He had accepted a new job in Atlanta and they were preparing to move! We went to a tapas restaurant that evening to celebrate Brad's resignation and new job, but poor little Henry was sick with a fever, and we ended up leaving the restaurant before most of the food had arrived. We got the food to-go and laughed about how it was the best "take-out" dinner we had ever had.

I left on Tuesday to return home—it was a whirlwind trip! When I arrived home, I was absolutely exhausted. I thought the trial drug might be causing fatigue along with major bouts of diarrhea. Speaking of which, I had been afraid to fly for fear of an accident on the plane, but I thanked Jesus for making it through each flight accident-free.

The summer was a busy but fulfilling time, full of family visits. Sean, Lindsey, and Cora came to visit for July 4th. Cora was so funny and ate everything in sight—I have never seen a little girl with such a huge appetite! She also learned to say Greg's and my grandparent names: Bubba and Cucu. She put an accent on the last syllable of Bubba, making it sound French. She had a bit more difficulty saying "Cucu," but it was coming along. "Cucu" means "grandmother" in Kikuyu, the language of the ethnic tribe I had worked with in Kenya. Although Cora had some difficulty saying "Cucu," she certainly knew who her Cucu was!

The day after Sean and Lindsey left, I had my first CT scan since starting the trial drug. Shortly thereafter, Greg and I went to Greenville to hear the results of the scan and find out whether or not the drug had been effective thus far. I went into my appointment feeling discouraged. I had a hunch that the medicine wasn't working. My stomach was sticking out even more, which had led me to believe the tumors were still growing rapidly. In fact, it was protruding so much I had to wear a tummy band.

Needless to say, I was pleasantly surprised to discover that the large tumor (by my right kidney) had only grown by eighteen percent (compared to 300 percent over the same timeframe prior to starting the trial). I was still eligible to stay on the trial. What's more, it looked like the other three tumors hadn't changed in size at all. I was immensely encouraged.

I was grateful for the path I was on; I was thankful that I could see how God was working out all the details; and I was hopeful because even if this drug didn't work, there were still two other trials available to me. Who but God could have aligned this? There wasn't just one clinical trial for rare tumors, but three clinical trials—all of which had the same genetic markers that my tumors had and all of which were based in Greenville. God is so good.

The doctor wanted me to stay on the trial drug for another cycle (three weeks), then have another CT scan, and then make decisions based on the information we received. My cancer was still growing, but the drug was slowing it down considerably. If the growth rate reached twenty percent or more, I would have to be taken off the trial. I got another three weeks' supply of the drug and we left the cancer center.

Both Greg and I were dumbstruck. It was hard to believe what we had seen and heard. We called Taylor to share the news with her and she, too, was dumbstruck. But once the news sank in, it was great. As evidenced, cancer is a roller coaster journey, replete with ups and downs, highs and lows, mountains and valleys. However, whenever I am in a valley, God is faithful to show me a glimmer of hope, giving me something to cling to and reminding me that He is in control.

Throughout this roller coaster journey, Greg has used the term "cautiously optimistic." On the other hand, I'm apt to say that I'm completely optimistic about the outcome because I know that the Lord is good and faithful.

## Day 689 – July 7, 2017

The summer was moving right along. Before I knew it, Greg and I were traveling to New York again, but this time for a special occasion: Henry's first birthday! Greg and I flew into the city on Friday morning and were the first family members to arrive for the weekend. Due to storms and flight delays, Ted and Gail (Brad's parents) as well as Dick (Taylor's dad) didn't arrive until late afternoon.

We helped out with Henry while Brad and Taylor ran errands in preparation for the birthday party. In the evening, we all met for dinner at one of Taylor's and Brad's favorite Italian restaurants, located near their first apartment. They hadn't been to the restaurant since Taylor's pregnancy, so that evening one of their favorite waitresses finally got to meet Henry! We had a wonderful meal and spent good family time together around the table.

After dinner, things took a turn for the worse. The side effects of my trial drug kicked into full gear, and I felt a diarrhea attack coming on. We paid the bill, left the restaurant, and walked down the street to hop in a taxi, but my stomach was cramping and I felt an urge. I rushed back to the restaurant, but nothing. As I exited, an Uber was just pulling up for Ted and Gail, and they graciously offered for Greg and me to take it. We hopped in and Greg asked the driver to take us back to our hotel as quickly as possible.

We had only driven ten blocks when the cramping became severe. I told Greg we needed to stop, but he told me to hang in there. We were only forty blocks from the hotel and we'd be there soon. As much as I wanted to be able to make it back to the hotel, I knew that I just couldn't. I insisted that we needed to stop—now! Greg realized I was serious and we didn't have a minute to spare. He quickly gave our driver a rundown regarding my cancer, the trial medication I was on, and the unfortunate side effects I was experiencing. We needed a bathroom fast.

We were right in the middle of an intersection when our Uber driver pulled over and told me that I could try the bar on the corner or the pizza place next door. I took off running for the bar which was closest. I almost bumped over the bouncer at the door, but I had my eyes fixed on two bathroom doors at the rear of the bar. I tried the first door. It was locked. I tried the second and, praise be to God, it opened. I reached the bathroom just in the nick of time.

When I emerged ten minutes later, sick and weak, I found Greg sitting at the bar. He had apologized to the bouncer and bought a beer while he waited for me. We left the bar to hail a taxi, but we discovered that our Uber driver was still waiting for us double parked! It was such a blessing to know that he didn't leave us in the midst of our dilemma. When we finally got back to our hotel, we thanked the driver and Greg gave him a very generous tip.

I was supposed to babysit Henry that night while everyone else decorated for the party, but I was far too sick and weak after that episode. Dick babysat Henry and I ended up going to bed, feeling horrible that I couldn't help!

Thankfully, I had recovered by the following day and was able to celebrate little Henry's first birthday. The rock n' roll-themed party went off without a hitch. Henry loves music, so Taylor hired a musician to sing and play with the children. And, of course, Henry had his smash cake. After the party, we cleaned up and cooked out on the patio, enjoying a quiet and relaxing night.

The next morning, we all dressed in blue and white to take family photos. We lunched at Tavern on the Green, and then all the extended family members left that afternoon. Greg and I went to church with Taylor, Brad, and Henry; then we left for the airport.

It was such a special weekend, but I was quite tired by the end of it. It's a struggle to handle normal life with cancer, especially when dealing with the side effects of a trial drug. As I look back on that rough night, I realize how God worked out all the little details. He even had a toilet ready for me at the exact moment I needed it. I choose to see His hand in the details. I choose to be thankful for the little things. I choose to trust Him.

# Day 707 – July 25, 2017

At the end of July, I had my three-week follow-up appointment with my oncologist specialist to evaluate the effectiveness of the trial drug. He was unable to pull up my most recent CT scan, but he had a copy of the report. The news he shared floored me—and not in a good way.

The three smaller tumors hadn't changed much in size, but the large tumor over my kidney had grown over twenty-five percent in the past three weeks, indicating progression of the cancer. This meant that I would have to be pulled off of the clinical trial. I was shocked because I had been feeling so healthy.

We began chatting about the next steps, and the specialist advised radiating the large tumor and then trying the immunotherapy trial. However, radiating the tumor could negatively affect my kidney, and there was no guarantee that radiation would kill the tumor completely. Likely, it would kill most of the tumor, the "leftovers" would become supercharged, and then the cancer cells would probably respond well to immunotherapy. The specialist concluded by saying that this was an "ideal" situation. I thought that was an odd thing to say. Nothing about this situation felt "ideal." I left his office feeling numb.

Still, in spite of this discouraging news, I chose to see God's hand in the details. I was eligible for the immunotherapy trial, which actually had great success of curing the cancer completely, and if immunotherapy didn't work, there were still two other options I could try. What's more, the doctors were amazed at how healthy I looked and felt even as I continued treatments. The three small tumors hadn't changed in size at all, which meant that the medicine *was* working, just not within the protocol. Perhaps the best news was that I would get to see more of my radiation oncologist.

When I met with my radiation oncologist, she pulled up my most recent CT scan. What Greg and I saw made us cringe: the large tumor over my right kidney was huge! We knew it was about the size of a grapefruit, but it was scary to see it in proportion to my body. A large portion of my liver was displaced toward the left side of my body and my right kidney was pushed very low, stretching the blood vessel that attaches to the vena cava.

All of my doctors agreed on the prognosis: radiation wouldn't kill the whole tumor. It was too large for standard radiation to have an effect. It was likely that radiation would kill part of the tumor and the remaining cancer cells would be supercharged from radiation, making them susceptible to immunotherapy, the "big buzz" treatment, as the specialist had informed us. My radiation oncologist wondered if surgery (to remove all or some of the tumor) would be an option and planned to discuss that with my two oncologist surgeons. In the meantime, I would have a body cast made and plan to start radiation the next Thursday, unless something changed.

I had just met with my counselor the day before my appointment to find out if the trial was working. I told her that I was feeling good and healthy, but despite that, I had the recurring thought that God wasn't through using this cancer not only as a way for me to testify to His glory but also to get Greg's attention.

I desperately want Greg to know Jesus as I do. All this pain and suffering would be so worth it. Even though I had been caught off guard by the news, I had sensed that this journey wasn't over yet. I continued to pray, asking God to reveal himself to Greg and to continue softening Greg's heart. I know that God has heard my prayers and that it is His will that all come to know Him.

At the end of July, I received an email from the associate pastor, Tony, at my church, asking if I could stop by so that he could pray over me. We spent an hour together sharing stories. I talked about how the Holy Spirit had been so present in my life and how God had been at work in all the details of this cancer journey. There were tears in his eyes when he finished praying over me, and he shared with me how much my faith had touched him. I praised God that my faithfulness could impact a pastor.

# Working Through
# the Darkness

# Day 713 – July 31, 2017

I'm so grateful that God works out my schedule so that I can be present for important events in my children's lives. As I mentioned, Taylor and Brad were moving to Atlanta, and I was so happy to be able to help with their move. We planned for me to fly to New York to help pack up the last few things and then fly to Atlanta with Taylor, Henry, and their cat while Brad drove the moving truck down.

I didn't sleep well the night before my 6:30am flight to New York, so Monday morning (my first day in the city) was rough. Once at the airport, I hopped in a cab and quickly discovered that my cab driver was a fanatical Muslim who preached to me about Allah, telling me that I needed to pray to Allah in order to go to heaven. I didn't hesitate to tell him that I was a Christian, that I pray to God every day, and that I know in my heart I'm going to heaven. The conversation quickly became fanatical and I felt suppressed, unable to speak strongly about my faith. What was usually a thirty minute drive from the airport into the city turned into a one hour and fifteen minute ride because the driver wasn't paying attention and continually made wrong turns.

He tried to convince me to read the Koran, specifically the first chapter, which is on healing. He even went so far as to begin playing a reading of the first chapter of the Koran on his phone. I asked him to please stop and take me to my hotel; I also told him that I had cancer and was very bothered. Then, he began praying to Allah for healing, asking Allah to open my eyes to the truth. I replied, quite determinately, that I know the truth. At last, he could see that I was getting very frustrated and he turned off the meter.

Finally, we arrived at my hotel. The driver said that he would wait until I checked in to take me to Taylor's apartment, but I declined his offer and said that I would walk. My room wasn't ready, but I dropped off my luggage and proceeded to walk the twenty-five blocks to Taylor's apartment to clear my head.

I arrived at Taylor's at about 10am and was amazed at how empty the apartment already was. Brad's friends from church were helping him load the truck and a babysitter was helping with Henry. After a few minutes, the babysitter took Henry to an art class and I walked back to my hotel to get settled in and ensure there was a crib in the room for Henry.

As I was walking back in the ninety degree heat, I received a phone call from Dr. E. He and my radiation oncologist were concerned that radiation could destroy my organs surrounding the tumor, and he suggested I try surgery first. We scheduled an appointment for me to see a urologist surgeon who would assist the oncology surgeon. The goal was to remove the large tumor, follow up with radiation, and then possibly try immunotherapy.

And so, here I was walking down Broadway in blisteringly hot weather, sweating profusely (so much so that I had to shake the sweat out of my phone in order to hear Dr. E.), and discussing my upcoming surgery. In the midst of all of this I was rudely interrupted by a girl asking me for money. When I explained that I was on the phone with my doctor, she began yelling at me and said that I was faking the call! I made my escape and continued speaking with Dr. E. I asked him a lot of questions and we had a good conversation about this change in direction.

I finally arrived at the hotel and checked in. My favorite desk clerk was there, and she was happy to see me again. I had stayed at the same hotel during all of my visits to New York, and it was such a joy to get to know some of the people who worked there. I told Mary that this would likely be my last trip to New York because my daughter was moving to Atlanta.

Not long after I checked in, the babysitter arrived with Henry. I put Henry down for his nap and tried to nap myself, but I couldn't fall asleep. So many thoughts were whirling through my mind. I was deeply concerned about Greg's faith, and I sensed the Holy Spirit pressing on my heart just how hard Greg's heart is to crack. I felt like it would take more than cancer to bring about change in him—possibly resurrecting me after dying on the operating table! (Actually, I was having a strange vision of flat-lining.) In light of my upcoming surgery, Taylor and I both felt a sense of urgency to talk to Greg.

Around 4:30 that afternoon, Taylor arrived at the hotel after dropping off the cat at the vet. We went out for burgers and treated Henry to his last ice cream with rainbow sprinkles from the Mr. Softee ice cream truck. Then, we went back to Taylor's apartment to clean it and retrieve the last few remaining things. Back at the hotel, I bathed Henry and put him to bed so that Taylor could go to a yoga class and then out for a glass of wine with her friend, Jade. I tossed and turned most of the night, getting only about six hours of sleep.

The following day was a whirlwind. We woke up early around 5:30am so that Taylor could get coffee and see the sun rise over the city one last time. New York City holds a special place in Taylor's heart. I knew she was excited to move to Atlanta to be close to family, especially during this time of illness, but I also knew she and Brad would miss this place dearly.

Over breakfast, I shared with Taylor about my Muslim taxi driver and how I had tossed and turned the night before with nightmarish thoughts about denying Christ. God put it on Taylor's heart to say that maybe God had put me in a situation where it was nearly impossible to share the Gospel in order to demonstrate how easy it would be to share with Greg.

The conversation then turned to a more difficult topic. Taylor told me that she felt like I had been acting more self-centered lately. She had a lot on her heart that she wanted to share and likely wanted the comfort of her mom, but instead she felt that all I talked about was the difficulties I was having with cancer. From my perspective, I was just trying to catch her up quickly since we never seem to have enough time together. It was a tough discussion, but also a much needed one to clear the air. This goes back, again, to how people respond to cancer. It is hard to understand what is truly going on within us. As much as I didn't want cancer to define me, it had taken over my life.

Most people know me as being selfless and putting others first, and I know Taylor does too, so this conversation was hard. I know that I need to take care of myself, but that doesn't give me an excuse to forget others and their needs. Taylor graciously pointed out that Jesus thought of others, not himself, even when he was dying on the cross. I always appreciate when Taylor speaks to me in truth and love. I know that with the Lord's help I can change. I am not the only one with cancer or a major affliction.

Honestly, no one (except other cancer patients) knows what it's like to have cancer and how it affects you. I realized that I need people to tell me how they see me acting. I say things in ways that don't necessarily come out right. I know I am not the same person I was before the diagnosis. I have a new normal now, and sometimes I don't like it, but I do accept it. I can attest to the fact that I have little to no memory, courtesy of chemo brain!

After breakfast, we took Henry to play in the fountain at Lincoln Center. Taylor left to purchase dry ice for her large supply of frozen breast milk that we needed to bring on the flight to Atlanta, and I took Henry back to the hotel to nap and pack. Taylor returned with a cooler, dry ice, and her frozen breast milk; she grabbed the cat carrier and dashed out to pick up the cat at the vet where it had been boarded during the packing process.

By 11am, Taylor arrived back at the hotel. She nursed Henry, showered, packed, and we were in a taxi heading to the airport by 11:45am. We had to get to the airport by 12:15pm in order to check the cooler with dry ice for our 1pm flight, but we missed the cut off time by three minutes!

Taylor ran in to get priority help (for the frozen breast milk), while I took everything up to the counter. With two suitcases, a cooler, a stroller, a cat carrier, a car seat, and a diaper bag, we looked like pack rats! Then, we hit another roadblock: the Delta agent wouldn't allow Taylor to check the frozen breast milk because she didn't have a receipt showing the poundage for the dry ice.

It was now 12:30pm, and we needed to make decisions quickly. It was mandatory for Taylor to be on the 1pm flight in order to make it to the vet's office in Atlanta to board the cat by 5pm. We decided that Taylor should fly without me, taking Henry, the cat, the stroller, the car seat, the diaper bag, and her purse, leaving me at the airport with two suitcases and a cooler full of breast milk.

Taylor was whisked away to catch the 1pm flight, and I was left standing at the desk hardly knowing what had happened and what to do next. I looked at the Delta agent and couldn't help but cry. The whole reason I had come to New York was to help Taylor with Henry and the cat on the flight, and (though it wasn't my fault) I couldn't even do that! But God was faithful to orchestrate everything in His timing.

One of the Delta agents told me I would have to fly standby on the next flight, but another agent was able to book a seat for me on the next flight departing at 2pm, and she only charged me for one bag. However, the dry ice and breast milk still posed a problem. Even without the receipt, the agent couldn't make an exception and check it because it wasn't in a ventilated cooler. The only option was to carry it on. To accomplish this, I had to remove all the frozen breast milk, dump the dry ice into a bag, put the milk back in the cooler, and then buy regular ice for the cooler once I had gone through security.

While I was working with the Delta agents, I began sharing my cancer story, explaining how special it was for me to be in New York to help Taylor move, especially since I was probably having surgery next week. As I shared my story, one of the agents teared up.

Finally, my predicament was sorted out, and the Delta agent kindly escorted me to the front of the TSA security line, which was nearly one hundred people deep. I began taking off my shoes and putting everything on the security belt, but again I was escorted to the front of the scanner line. I sent the milk through and then met with the security manager on the other side for him to inspect it.

Once I had made it through security, I stopped at Starbucks to buy ice for the cooler. Funnily enough, the barista at Starbucks thought I was selling the breast milk! I explained my situation and she filled the cooler with ice free of charge. Afterward, I had five minutes to spare before boarding—just enough time call Greg. I ended up in seat 13A on a thirty-nine row plane. This was a pleasant surprise considering I almost had to fly standby!

In the end, everything worked out perfectly aside from the fact that I wasn't able to help Taylor with Henry and the cat. We rendezvoused at the hotel in Atlanta before going out for dinner and relaxing over a glass of wine. I thanked the Lord for working out the details not only in my life, but also in the lives of Taylor and Brad. God cares about even the smallest details of our lives!

## Day 719 – August 6, 2017

When I returned home to Seneca, I went back to LifePoint, the new church I had been attending recently, where I ran into my friend Alicia. I told her about my upcoming surgery, and she prayed over me. After church, I went for a walk and ran into Lynda. I also gave Lynda an update on my cancer and upcoming surgery, and she sent me an encouraging podcast to listen to. I love it when God puts people in front of me when I need them most.

Then, I went by the Cancer Center to see my chemo nurse, April, and to let her know about my upcoming surgery. April said that she would continue to keep me in her prayers. When I saw my counselor, I told her about the vision I had had of flat lining on the operating table. My counselor seemed so fascinated by my faith journey that I sometimes wondered if God was using me to increase her faith. If that was the case, I can only thank the Lord for using me and my story for His glory.

Friday, August 11 was the greatly anticipated day of surgery. The night before, Taylor and I spoke about the possibility of my death, and we even began planning my funeral. We discussed having the celebration of life at the cross on the lake and listed all the songs we wanted to be played. Taylor thought it would be a good idea to give away the charm I had been wearing since my cancer diagnosis—the one with the inscription, "*It is well with her soul.*" Ultimately, we decided that my funeral should be a celebration of my life. We talked about who would conduct the funeral and how I wanted Taylor to speak. We shed a few tears together, then we put the plans on the shelf and realized that we needed to trust Jesus with my life.

# Day 724 – August 11, 2017

On Friday, Greg and I arrived at the hospital at 10:30am for my 1:30pm surgery. Taylor, Brad, Henry, Sean, John, and Rhonda all showed up to spend time with me before the surgery. I loved having Henry sit on my hospital bed with me during pre-op. Alicia (my friend from church) had told me that Pastor Jud was going to pray over me prior to my surgery, but he was flying in from abroad and was unsure if he would make it in time. Another pastor showed up, thinking Jud wouldn't make it, and he prayed over me just before I received my epidural.

After I was given the epidural and some pain meds, the family came in to say their goodbyes. Apparently, I said some pretty stupid things while under the influence of the pain medication. Just before I was wheeled off to the operating room, Pastor Jud arrived and prayed over me, praying that the doctors would have wisdom during surgery.

This next part is based on what several people have told me (since I was under anesthesia in the operating room). Approximately thirty minutes after the surgery had started, the surgeon paged Greg and asked him to gather the family in the conference room. He then went back to the OR, and the family sat in silence for ten minutes, waiting. What do you do when you find yourself in "the wait?" Those are great opportunities to spend volumes of time on one's knees. We are not alone in "the wait;" He is with us. There is nobody I would rather wait with than Him. It is in that "wait" that we discover the strength we never had before. I believe sometimes God makes us for "the wait" and for the work that it accomplishes in us.

Taylor asked Greg if this had ever happened before during my previous surgeries. He said it hadn't. I can't imagine what was going through everyone's minds, especially since I had expressed concern that I would flatline on the operating table. The surgeon arrived in the conference room, noted "it's never good when you see me," and explained what was going on. When they cut me open, they found tumors in my liver and discovered that my mesentery (which covers my intestines) was covered in 1 cm tumors. The surgeons felt that if they tried to remove the large tumor above my right adrenal gland—at the risk of nicking my vena cava—they would also have to take my right kidney and part of my liver. Even then, they still wouldn't be able to remove all the cancer.

If they were to proceed, I would be looking at a four-week recovery time at best, which would delay any further treatment. The surgeon explained that he had discussed the situation with Dr. E. and collectively they made the decision to leave everything as is and sew me back up so a systemic treatment could start quickly.

Like I said, it is during the wait that we discover we are not alone. We find God with us and we become warriors. During this time, two of my friends showed up at the hospital. One of them had a strong feeling that she was there for Greg and asked if she could pray over him. Greg reluctantly consented. As my friend was praying, she felt a tremendous amount of darkness in the room, but she continued in prayer, feeling the presence of God arise.

When I woke up in the hospital room later, I received the disappointing news that the surgeons had elected not to proceed with removing the cancer. But I praised God for answered prayers and that they didn't proceed, knowing the risk of nicking the vena cava and possibly bleeding out. On Saturday afternoon, an assistant to my surgeon came in and told me that he had been in the operating room during my procedure. He was sorry that there was nothing he could do about my cancer, but he told me it was now his job to get me back on my feet as soon as possible so that I could start chemo to kill the cancer. He wore a pin on his lapel that said, "Ask and I will pray for you." He also wore a big smile on his face.

I, too, wanted to get back on my feet as soon as possible, and I had my epidural removed so that Greg and Sean could start walking me around. But due to the pain medication, I could hardly walk. On Sunday, I had them take me off the pain meds and I was able to walk by that afternoon. As I turned a corner, I literally bumped into Sandra, my good friend from Raleigh. She had been in Asheville and stopped in to see me before returning home. What a sweet surprise! Another friend of mine from Raleigh, Becky, stopped in on the way to Atlanta. What a gift that God would put these people in my life.

I also received a surprise visit from my radiation oncologist on Monday. She told me how she and her husband had wondered why God would allow me to be opened up on the operating table only to be sewn back up without having the cancer removed. Her husband believed that it happened this way so that when God heals me, no one can deny how full of cancer I had been!

Dr. E. and his team came by to discuss my prognosis. If things continued to progress as is, without being able to stop the tumor growth, I might have a week or a month, but at most I would be lucky to be alive at Christmas. Dr. E. suggested I speak with hospice, and we also discussed my options moving forward. He wanted to take a systemic approach and try Ifosfamide—the "last resort" chemo. Greg and I spoke about it and agreed that I was in good hands and that we should move forward with his treatment plan.

My port for chemo was put in on Tuesday and then I left the hospital that evening, knowing that I would have to return in a week for my first round of Ifosfamide. The first round is administered in the hospital due to the bad side effects: blood in the urine and possible hallucinations. I would need to be watched around the clock for three days. This gave me one week at home to recover from surgery and get as healthy as possible before beginning chemo.

## Day 731 – August 18, 2017

Taylor, Brad, and Henry arrived on Thursday to help take care of me. Much of the family was coming in for the weekend to visit and witness the total eclipse of the sun (the path went right over our lake house!). Sean, Lindsey, Cora, Nikki, John, and Rhonda arrived on Saturday afternoon for the weekend. We had quite a full house with nine adults and two grandbabies.

Taylor was a huge blessing and completely took charge of the weekend. She did all the grocery shopping as well as planned and cooked all the meals. I was too weak to pick up either grandbaby, but I thoroughly enjoyed watching them play together as they jumped on the sofa, kissed each other, and walked hand in hand wherever they went.

Monday was the day of the total eclipse. We all went down to the dock and put on our special eclipse glasses. During the last ten minutes before totality, it kept getting darker and darker. Finally, it was so dark the cicadas came out. When totality hit, we took off our glasses and saw the ring of fire. Just as the sun started to peak out, it looked like a sparkling diamond solitaire. We were all awestruck. I had never seen anything like it! What a beautiful sight to see after the difficult valley I had been in.

## Day 735 – August 22, 2017

Spending the weekend with loved ones helped prepare me both mentally and emotionally for my first week of chemo. By Monday, I was finally getting stronger, and by Tuesday, I was back in the hospital for my first round of Ifosfamide.

I was admitted to the hospital around 11:30am, but the chemo didn't start until 5pm due to the rigmarole of paperwork, blood work, calculations for the right amount of chemo, and making the chemo in the pharmacy. The treatment was a seven-hour process for three days, which means I didn't finish each day until midnight. To make matters worse, I couldn't sleep each night due to the steroids I was given.

The nurse who administered my chemo was dressed in a hazmat suit. In fact, she even put a rubber pad on the floor for protection, claiming the treatment would eat a hole in the floor. I asked her if she were really going to put this poison in me, and she casually replied, "Of course! It kills cancer."

Thankfully, the three-day treatment was uneventful and free of any side effects. I also had several visitors to help pass the time. On Wednesday, my older brother brought our sister to visit me; it was her first visit since Greg and I had moved to South Carolina. They commented that I seemed quite healthy and, as always, I acknowledged that it was God who was giving me the strength to keep moving forward. In a way, it's unfortunate that they haven't really seen what I've gone through. I have a tendency to bounce back quickly so most people see me healthy and strong. My diagnosis can be very misleading since I don't seem like someone who is dying of cancer.

On Thursday, my friends Ann and Nan came for a three-hour visit. We went to the food court for a bite to eat, which was my first time out of my hospital room since starting chemo. In the food court, I ran into my surgeon's assistant, who was all smiles. He gave me a big hug and told me how happy he was to see me doing well.

The weekend after my first chemo treatment was one of recovery. The main aftermath was extreme tiredness. I didn't have the flu-like symptoms in my legs that I had experienced during my other chemo, but I was so tired that I napped twice daily. My friend Alicia picked me up to go to church on Sunday since I was still too weak to drive. But it felt so good to be back in church, worshipping the Lord.

Taylor, Brad, and Henry came to visit over Labor Day weekend. Taylor and I drove to Greenville to go shopping, and we had a great conversation while sitting in the car in the parking garage, waiting for Henry to wake up. We discussed my care and how Taylor is taking time off of work to help care for me. On Saturday, Taylor and Brad went running while I watched Henry. He fell asleep in my arms and slept for an hour while I sat on the front porch swing. It was a taste of heaven! A gentle breeze was blowing, the sky was blue, and my grandson was sleeping in my arms. Later that day, we went for a boat ride and Henry fell asleep in my arms again. I'm such a blessed grandmother.

That weekend I also received a text from Dr. E. with my CA125 number. Before my surgery, the number was 232; after only one chemo treatment, my CA125 had dropped to 132. This was a significant drop, and it indicated that the chemo was working and maybe the small tumors had died.

After my tox check with Dr. E. (to ensure all was well for the second round of chemo), I took off by myself to drive to Atlanta. I wanted nothing more than to go and love on Henry! I let myself into Taylor's and Brad's apartment, and when they returned in the evening and Henry caught sight of me, he squealed with delight and ran to me with open arms.

It was a wonderful weekend. Brad's mom, Gail, also came for a night, and she and I took Henry out to dinner so that Brad and Taylor could have a date night. On Friday, we spent time at the art museum, where Henry had story time and worked on an art project. Taylor and I also took Henry to the botanical gardens for kid's music time; we played on the playground at Piedmont park; and we went to the farmer's market. By the end of the weekend, I was worn out but in a good way. My heart was full.

# Day 755 – September 11, 2017

Prior to round two of chemo, I had gone back to yoga to work on my balance and strength. I think it helped because I made it through the second round with flying colors. I walked each day after I left the treatment center at 4pm, which also seemed to help. I returned to yoga the day after I concluded the week's chemo, thankful for the desire to remain strong. I am always thankful that God gave me the desire to exercise, to keep pushing. I have sensed that this physical strength that I am able to maintain will allow the doctors to continue to try additional therapies on me. I have high hopes that they will either be able to find a cure for this cancer through me or at least be able to manage it like a chronic disease.

I also realized that if I can muster up just enough energy to stay even slightly active during chemo, the side effects aren't as bad. Over the weekend I spent time on the boat and sweated in the sauna to detox—probably a good idea since the chemo is so toxic!

I needed to get strong as quickly as possible because I was leaving for a trip with Taylor that upcoming Thursday. When Sunday rolled around I was feeling very weak, but I was determined to get up and drive myself to church.

My pastor had started a new series on spiritual warfare, and the teaching centered on Daniel and his focus on God. Daniel didn't give up praying until God sent an angel to him, but it took the angel twenty-one days to get to Daniel because he had been detained. Pastor Blake was sharing about the importance of remaining focused on the Lord and to continue praying in times of trouble. We don't know God's timing or when and how He may answer our prayers. Blake then began telling the story of a woman with incurable cancer who exudes Christ. I suddenly realized he was talking about me! I was extremely humbled and teared up. I had no idea he was going to speak about my situation. After the service, a college student from Clemson approached me and shared that her dad had cancer. She said that my story inspired her and gave her hope.

God laid it on my heart to share the video of the sermon with Greg and my prayer warriors. I believed that God knew just who needed to hear the story and how it would touch their lives. Later Sunday evening, I had a chance to reflect on what had happened. Two and a half years ago, just before we left Raleigh, I was diagnosed with cancer, and I fully believed then (as I do now) that God allowed it to happen for His glory. I shared this with my pastor, and I thought it might come up in one of his sermons, but it wasn't the Lord's timing. Then, we moved to Seneca, and I started attending another church. Someone mentioned that I should talk to the pastor about sharing my cancer story with the congregation, but again I felt it wasn't the Lord's timing.

Then, when I least expected it (and without my knowledge), my pastor at LifePoint Church shared my story. By that time, God had used me for His glory in so many ways, my story had more detail, and the outcome was something only God could have orchestrated.

I read the following in my devotional by Oswald Chambers: "God rarely allows a person to see how great a blessing he is to others" (Chambers, September 6). As I thought about this, I realized how much it makes sense. If God allowed us to see how He's using us, it would likely go to our heads and inflate our egos. We might start thinking, "Look what I've done," instead of giving God the praise and pointing others to Him.

I know that we are created to glorify God, and it is my desire to give God all the glory for not only using me to bless others, but also giving me the strength to endure this suffering. I've mentioned before how often people comment on my strength throughout this trial, and I strive to continually give God the glory because He gives me the strength to carry on.

# Choosing Joy in Times of Sorrow

# Day 765 – September 21, 2017

After my surgery in August, I truly felt my death may be drawing near. It was important for Taylor and me to spend some quality time together, making memories and loving on each other, so we planned a trip to California. Thursday finally rolled around, and I set off for Atlanta to meet Taylor and begin our trip. We had planned to leave after my second round of chemo, knowing by then how the chemo would affect me.

However, God had other plans—even better plans. I love how He writes the master plan of our lives and knows every step, for He orders them. He always seems to thwart my human plans to show me something even greater. On my drive to Atlanta, I received a call from Hillary, Dr. E.'s nurse, who shared my updated CA125. Three weeks ago, my CA125 had dropped to 132, now it was only forty! The chemo was obviously working, and the cancer was dying. What began as an "end of life" trip turned into a "celebration of life" trip.

Taylor had planned an amazing trip to California. We flew into San Francisco and visited with a friend of Taylor's who took us sailing on the San Francisco Bay. Then we ate dinner at a wonderful sushi restaurant. For breakfast the next morning, we ended up at a tourist attraction called Mama's, but it was well worth the two-hour wait! Taylor and I ordered three breakfasts for the two of us and ate everything!

On Saturday afternoon, we drove to Napa Valley and checked into our hotel. When the receptionist realized I had cancer, we were upgraded to a suite. We then drove up to Calistoga where we had reservations for a volcanic ash mud bath, which was an amazing experience. The following day, we spent the morning getting spa treatments before setting off on our first wine tour of a small boutique winery. The next morning we hiked, biked, and found a famous bakery that's one of Oprah Winfrey's favorite places; we also went to two wineries that afternoon.

Interestingly, there was a picture of a pruned grapevine in our hotel room, which is significant to both Taylor and me. It reminded me of one of my favorite verses, "I am the vine; you are the branches; if you remain in me and I in you, you will bear much fruit; apart from me you can do nothing" (*NIV*, John 15:5), and also, "He cuts off every branch in me that bears no fruit, while every branch that does bear fruit he prunes so that it will be even more fruitful" (*NIV*, John 15:2).

I was so excited about the picture that I asked the front desk to locate the artist for me. After I returned home, I tracked down the artist. I shared with him my cancer story and what his picture meant to me. He had never taken a personal order for his artwork (he only sold it for commercial use), but he was touched and took my order for two prints. Once I received them, he even advised me how to have them framed and wished me well with my cancer. One now hangs over my bed and the other I gave to Taylor for her birthday in October as a reminder of this beautiful trip and the significance that it had on our lives and in our memories.

Taylor and I had so much fun together that we didn't want the trip to end. However, when we returned to Atlanta, we had the sweet surprise of seeing Henry take his first steps across the room!

# Day 777 – October 3, 2017

During round three of chemo, I walked every day to minimize the side effects. The pastors from my old church came to visit, and the Lord placed it on my heart to tell them that I was leaving their church to go where I felt the Lord had now called me. It was a difficult decision, but it was important for me to be obedient to the Lord. I had been called to their church for a purpose and I felt that I had fulfilled what God had placed on my heart. Now it was time for me to move forward.

After round three of chemo, I went to Michigan with Greg to visit his 95-year-old father. His father had been in the hospital with pneumonia and was coughing up blood. We realized that he wouldn't be able to come down to the lake and see our new home, so it was important for us to go see how he was doing and help make decisions regarding his care. Greg's brother also came to Michigan for the weekend, and we enjoyed family time together. No one there had seen me since I had been diagnosed with cancer, and I believe it did them good to see how well I was doing.

I returned from Michigan and had my nadir check. My CA125 was now down to twenty-nine (thirty is within normal range). I also saw my CT scan results, and it appeared as though the large tumor above my adrenal gland was changing consistency. This was a good sign it might be dying. The small tumors that covered my mesentery didn't show up on the CT scan, meaning they were likely dead since my CA125 count was so low.

I felt as though I had been given a second chance at life. I felt as though God was healing me. Dr. E. decided to wait until after round six of chemo to do the next CT scan and see what was happening to the tumors.

## Day 793 – October 19, 2017

I had been waiting for Thursday, October 19 for a month. This was the day that Lydiah, one of my "daughters" in Kenya, was arriving for an overnight visit. I had met Lydiah and her husband, Francis, while doing short-term mission work in Kenya with Freedom Global. Freedom Global is a Christian non-profit organization that works with the poorest of the poor in the Rift Valley outside of Nairobi in Kenya. These people were burned out of their homes in the post-election violence of 2007. Freedom Global, under the direction of the co-founder and CEO, Brad, has gone in and restored dignity to these people by building a village and creating jobs so that families can be taken care of. Mud huts were contructed in place of tent villages, wells were dug, and greenhouses were built to grow vegetables to sell to local restaurants.

Over the years, Freedom Global has created additional job opportunities for locals by building a pig farm, growing wheat and corn, and, more recently, creating a dairy farm that has become a huge success. The profits generated by these businesses enabled Freedom Global to open their first all-girls boarding school to educate the young girls from these villages—girls who would never have received an education past primary school. Because it's a Christian school, the girls attend Bible study, and many have come to know the Lord.

Both Lydiah and her husband had come to the U.S. for the first time several years ago for a fundraiser for Freedom Global, and now Lydiah was returning on her own to speak at churches and help raise funds to continue this work in Kenya. Three years had passed since I had last seen Lydiah. When Brad pulled up in my driveway, Lydiah jumped out of the car and hugged me so tightly she actually lifted me off the ground. We were both grinning from ear to ear.

We took a tour of the house and then spent time on the dock overlooking the lake and catching up on our lives. Lydiah had brought touching letters from her husband, Francis, for Greg and me. We took Lydiah to dinner on the lake at the Lighthouse, and she ordered salmon—her favorite fish that isn't available in Kenya. In fact, she ate salmon every night for dinner while in the United States!

The next morning, we met with missionaries from church and shared what Freedom Global does. As it turns out, those missionaries had spent time in Kenya and even shared mutual friends with Lydiah. I'm always so fascinated to see God at work. There are no coincidences in life and He plans all the details!

Lydiah had to leave after lunch and prayer, and we were both sad to see the visit end. I hope to be well enough to return to Kenya and continue the work we have been doing! She and Francis mean so much to me; it is through them that God taught me about sacrificial giving and loving your neighbor.

## Day 798 – October 24, 2017

I was dreading round four of chemo. Just when I would start feeling good and healthy, I'd have to go in for another round of chemo, which involved sitting for seven to eight hours a day for three consecutive days and then feeling exhausted for several days afterward.

I felt as though I lost a week of my life every three weeks. Usually, I would go for a walk on the first two days after chemo, but then I would spend the third day sleeping since I was just too exhausted to do anything. This chemo treatment is supposed to be one of the hardest to handle, and it was starting to wipe me out. I was experiencing shortness of breath, and I was even having a difficult time climbing the stairs for several days after a treatment round.

During this fourth round of chemo, I received a beautiful reminder from a friend: "This sickness will not end in death. No, it is for God's glory so that God's Son may be glorified through it" (*NIV*, John 11:4). This scripture has been one I've been holding in my heart throughout my cancer journey. It was interesting to me that the Lord also brought it to someone else's mind. I love how God works and repeats important things.

After this round of chemo, I took a trip to Atlanta to see Henry. I always try to go down on the third week when I feel the healthiest. I read in my Jesus Calling devotional, "Learn to appreciate the difficult days. Be stimulated by the challenges you encounter along your way. As you journey through rough terrain with Me, gain confidence from your knowledge that together we can handle anything" (Young, p.327). I realized how down I had gotten during my last chemo. I was dwelling on my circumstances and not on God. So, I decided to change my attitude and look forward to the next chemo, knowing that God was using it to heal me. I will continue to praise Him and give Him thanks for all He has done and is doing.

I have been thinking about and wondering how the Lord will use me when I'm healed from cancer. I've felt so close to Jesus over the past two years. He has been my constant companion and strength—and I don't want to lose that. If it's better to continue having cancer so that He can be glorified through it, I am fine with that. I am open to what He has planned; after all, He is in control. Lately though, I've felt a nudging from the Lord to write my book and finish it to be prepared for my next journey.

I had a doctor's appointment for a tox check prior to round five of chemo. While I was in Greenville for the blood test, I stopped in to see my radiation oncologist. She told me about a women's conference she was planning for May 2018 and how she felt like the Lord had prompted her to ask me if I would consider speaking at the conference. Maybe this is what God has planned for me next. I told her that if it was the Lord's will, I would love to do it.

I felt very positive about going into my fifth round of chemo. I trusted that God had begun the healing process. My cousin, Susan, had recently moved to North Carolina from New Jersey, so she came to visit me, bringing her brother, Dave, with her. We had both lost our moms somewhat recently, and we realized that we are now the "old" generation.

During her visit, Susan shared how she had put my update emails in chronological order and had sent them to her sister-in-law in upstate New York. Her sister-in-law, in turn, shared my emails with her church and told Susan that they were all praying for me. She was also hoping to share them with a cousin of hers who has cancer and is not in a good place and needs some encouragement. The timing wasn't right but I knew God would put on her heart the perfect timing to share. I'm amazed at how far and wide my faith story has traveled, especially to people I don't know—it is truly a work of God!

Round five of chemo was going well. On Wednesday, Dr. E.'s nurse, Hillary, came to chat and share stories with me. When I told her that I was going to start writing my book, she prayed over me, my book, and the people my book would touch.

On Sunday, November 19, the husband of one of my good friends passed away. He had prostate cancer that had metastasized to his bones. He underwent five rounds of chemo, which seemed to stop the cancer growth, but then he died of congestive heart failure. Cancer weakens its patients and causes a host of other issues. I've often heard that people with cancer don't necessarily die of cancer, but instead die from complications related to the host of other issues that the cancer and treatments cause. My friend's husband was a great man with a wonderful sense of humor. It made me realize how close to death I have been and how easily that could have been me. Each day is a gift from God, and I hope I can learn to better appreciate each day, living life to the fullest.

# Day 828 – November 23, 2017

Thanksgiving of 2017 marked my 828th day of cancer. I remembered the prior Thanksgiving, holding hands with my family in the kitchen as I said the blessing and praised the Lord that I had been healed. Fast forward one year: I had undergone three more surgeries and additional treatments. However, I still thanked God for healing me in His perfect timing. What's more, we were blessed with news from Sean and Lindsey that they were expecting their second child, due in May. I was thrilled to have a third grandchild on the way.

After Thanksgiving, I had a CT scan on Tuesday and then went to Greenville on Thursday to hear the results. The oncologist reviewed the report and relayed the disheartening news: there was no significant change in the size of the tumors from the last scan. I called Taylor and cried. She tried to find the silver lining, pointing out that although the tumors hadn't shrunk, they also hadn't grown, and there were no new ones. Perhaps I was reaching a point of "maintenance mode" where chemo was keeping everything at bay. But the thought of having chemo treatments every three weeks for the rest of my life was highly unappealing.

When I arrived home from Greenville, there was a package waiting for me on the porch. I glanced at the address label and didn't recognize the handwriting. I also noticed that the return address was a New York address. With no idea who it was from, I opened the package to find a teddy bear from my cousin's sister-in-law, who lives in upstate New York. Her church, which had been praying for me for months, had prayed over the teddy bear and sent it to me to comfort me in times of sorrow. What providential timing. Again, God met me in my valley and comforted me.

Round six of chemo, during the first week of December, went well. I met a new cancer patient who had colon cancer, pancreatic cancer, and cancer in her skull. She was on several different chemo treatments and had a strong will to live for her two-year-old. She didn't even want to know her prognosis. Instead, she trusted God that she would be healed.

Dr. E. told me that he wanted to do at least eight rounds of Ifosfamide. The tumors were changing, he thought, so he felt I should continue with the treatments. After eight rounds, I'd have a CT scan, and then we'd make further decisions. Dr. E. was surprised at how well I was doing with the Ifosfamide treatments. Ifosfamide—an older chemo discovered in the 1960's and approved in the 1980's—is supposedly a really bad chemo, but I hadn't experienced any major side effects. I felt like Shadrach, Meshach, and Abednego in the book of Daniel when they were thrown into the fiery furnace. Just as Jesus was in the furnace with them, protecting them from the fire, I too felt Jesus protecting me from the harmful side effects of this chemo.

Shortly before Christmas, I had my six-month cleaning at the dentist. Teri (an office assistant) had a special vial of healing oil that she had miraculously been able to get her hands on. The oil came from a prayer room in Dalton, Georgia, where there is a Bible that continuously and inexplicable leaks oil. Teri was led by the Spirit to ask if she could anoint me with this special oil. So, while I was lying in the chair getting my teeth cleaned, she anointed my feet and forehead with crosses and prayed over me. When I returned home that afternoon, I went for a walk and listened to a sermon. I felt God lay Isaiah 61:1 on my heart. I believe that the Lord gave me the oil of gladness instead of mourning and a garment of praise instead of a spirit of despair.

Christmas came and went, and praise God I was still alive. I'm living on borrowed time, but aren't we all? Greg and I spent Christmas in Atlanta with Taylor, Brad, Henry, Gail and Ted. We prayed that 2018 would be the year that God would heal me of this cancer. It has been a difficult journey, without much letup.

Greg and his son planned a fishing trip to Florida for early January. I think it's good for Greg to get his mind off of me every once in a while. Dealing with cancer is cumulative, meaning it gets harder and harder; and I believe it's harder on the caregiver. I am thankful for the comfort I get from Christ, but for me, one of the most difficult things is that I don't have the energy to do what I want to do. It makes me sad that I can't be the energetic grandma that I want to be, and it's increasingly difficult to adjust to the new "me"—the cancer version of me.

## Day 867 – January 1, 2018

In the beginning of January, I suffered from a severe headache for over a week. This was unusual because I actually hadn't suffered from a migraine since receiving my cancer diagnosis. I spoke with Dr. E., who wanted to do a CT scan to rule out a tumor in my brain. I asked him if he had ever seen this type of cancer move to the brain; he had seen it happen to one patient, so another scan was scheduled.

We also discussed how many rounds of chemo I could go through before the cancer might mutate (eventually it would and the chemo would no longer be effective). Dr. E. said that one patient underwent ten rounds of chemo before the cancer mutated. I laughed and said that I would do a dozen—no, make that thirteen rounds for good measure. We scheduled for me to meet with Dr. E. again the following Tuesday to discuss clinical trials and next steps to prepare for the mutation. It's important that we're able to move quickly since this cancer is so aggressive.

On Sunday, my small group prayed over me for the results of my CT scan. The results showed no tumors in my brain! What was leading me into depression soon resulted in elation. But my elation was short-lived. In mid-January, I reached a low point of depression. It was then that the Lord laid it on my heart to stop focusing on my circumstances and focus on Him instead. I knew that my focus on Jesus was the reason why I was doing so well, so why didn't I continue to focus on Him? It is our sinful, human nature that makes us think about ourselves and our circumstances. Once we start down that self-centered path, Satan gladly helps us along and we can spiral out of control. I spent a long time in fervent prayer one night, and the next morning my depression was lifted.

On the second day of my eighth round of chemo, we had a terrible snowstorm and the infusion center was closed, which was virtually unheard of! The snowstorm was nothing short of a blessing in disguise because I had been nauseous and vomiting all night from the chemo and felt far too weak to go in the next morning. Once out of this eighth round, I began feeling better, and Greg and I decided to plan a vacation. I wanted to go somewhere warm, so we chose St. Lucia as our destination and made the arrangements.

We planned to leave once I had received my nadir check after my ninth round of chemo to confirm my blood levels were fine to travel. At that point, my counts should be on the upswing and I should have ten good days. I went to Atlanta to help with Henry the first week that Taylor went back to work. Unfortunately, Greg had gotten sick prior to my trip to Atlanta, and when I returned home, I started feeling sick as well. Since my immune system is compromised, it takes me much longer to get well, and I worried I wouldn't be well enough for our trip. Thankfully, I never ran a fever with my sickness and we were able to keep the trip to St. Lucia on schedule.

# Day 912 – February 15, 2018

On our trip, Greg and I stayed at an all-inclusive resort that offered daily fitness classes and spa treatments. Greg and I started each day together with an early breakfast, and then we went our separate ways. I would take several fitness classes, have a massage or facial, and then meet Greg for a healthy lunch by the beach. After lunch, we'd spend several hours by the pool, soaking up vitamin D, and then I'd end the day with sunset yoga. In the evenings, Greg and I would meet back up for a cocktail and go to dinner together.

We also took a beginning scuba class, a tour of volcanoes (which included a volcanic mud bath), and a half-day snorkeling tour. Greg and I celebrated our 22nd anniversary with a bottle of champagne and an oceanside five-course dinner. I returned home feeling healthier than I had ever felt since my diagnosis.

On the trip, I met several women who had breast cancer. They approached me because they knew I, too, had cancer. My bald head is a dead giveaway! I also met a young woman named Nicole who worked in the wellness center and had recently lost her sister to cancer. I met a man, Isaiah, whose wife had recurrent breast cancer and was having a difficult time with an upcoming surgery and additional treatments. I'm so thankful that the Lord uses me in my difficult circumstances to minister to others. I remained in contact with both Nicole and Isaiah, and I hope to go back to St. Lucia next year to see them.

The day after returning home, I jumped into round ten of chemo. Thankfully, I bounced back by Saturday and immediately started exercising to be strong for the bike ride with Taylor in New York the following weekend. For the past two years Taylor has ridden in Cycle For Survival, a charity bike ride to raise money for rare cancer research for Memorial Sloan Kettering. This year I was feeling healthy and asked Taylor if we could do it together. It's a four-hour event that takes place in multiple cities and states over a three month timeframe. This year, they raised over $39 million, and there were 34,000 total participants who rode 7,600 bikes across sixteen cities.

Taylor named our team "Light for Lucinda," and she not only plans to ride every year, but also to grow the team. During our ride, there was so much energy in the gym. Taylor had invited her New York friends to ride with us. Between one-hour rides, we heard from motivational speakers, doctors, and cancer patients. Their stories encouraged us to get back on our bikes and ride for another hour. One speaker had a very similar story to mine. She had been dealing with cancer for three years and had undergone multiple surgeries and treatments. After the event, I sought her out and we exchanged stories. This was the first woman I had ever met with a similar story. We exchanged information and promised to stay in touch and be a support to one another.

When I returned home from New York, I had another CT scan, and I received the results just prior to my trip to San Antonio with Rhonda. The results were good news! The large tumor over my right kidney had decreased in size by about twenty percent; one tumor in my liver had decreased in size down to .8 cm, and the other tumor in my liver was gone; the tumor in my lymph node had stayed the same at 1.4 cm.

I took off for San Antonio with Rhonda where we stayed on the Riverwalk. We had a great time sightseeing, touring, shopping, and eating as we celebrated the good news of my results. I trusted that Jesus was taking care of me and that He had already planned the next treatment for when the cancer mutates.

I returned from San Antonio to round eleven of chemo, but I got sick with a bad cold and had to cancel the last day of treatment because I was running a fever. It took me over a week to recover. I figured that I had probably done too much traveling and had worn myself down. When I had my nadir check, I discovered that my CA125 had gone up to 60, which we expected to happen eventually, due to the cancer mutating and likely growing.

In mid-April I had round twelve of chemo and I actually rebounded well. Lately, it seems that everywhere I turn I am blessed by others. A woman at the jewelry store, whom I had met only one time, told me she prays for me every day. There's a woman who I run into at the chemo infusion center on a regular basis and she also believes the Lord will heal her. She told me that her sister sees me wrapped in the wings of an angel who is protecting me. Every month or so, I meet a girlfriend to have lunch and pray together. Once, while having lunch in a quaint deli, the waitress approached us out of the blue and blessed me. She had been a meth addict, her house had burned down, her dad died, and then she and her husband were saved. She now witnesses to others about her faith and she prays daily that the Lord will place one person in her path each day to bless. I happened to be that person on that day.

In early May, I went to visit Taylor, Brad and Henry in Atlanta. While there, I needed to have a bracelet repaired at a jewelry store. The sales rep started a conversation with me (he knew I had cancer due to my bald head), and I shared my cancer story with him. He shared with me that an associate's wife has the exact same cancer. She was traveling from Charlotte to Atlanta for treatments. She has young children and has been fighting for three years. He asked if he could pass my contact information on to her in case she would like someone to talk with. Afterwards, the sales associate wanted to give me a hug; he was so amazed at my strength and my faith. He was a Muslim and had never met a Christian with so much faith. These are the moments that I now live for: seeing God's hand everywhere I turn.

# Facing the End

## Day 990 – May 5, 2018

I had been asked by my radiation oncologist to speak and give my testimony at a women's retreat in Winnsboro, South Carolina in May. Women came from all over South Carolina, about 160 in attendance. It was a weekend event, but I arrived on Saturday evening in time for dinner and the evening service. There I heard the keynote speaker who was a pastor from Tennessee. Hearing her speak made me nervous. She was so filled with the Spirit and was such an incredible speaker. I was to speak first thing Sunday morning. That night I prayed fervently for the Lord to take over when I gave my testimony, and I prayed that it would touch every woman there.

I had never done a lot of public speaking and I was asked to prepare a thirty-minute talk, but two days before the conference I was asked to speak for forty-five minutes instead of thirty. I let God take over and I spoke for an hour. I don't even remember what I said. But I do remember when I walked up on stage and look out at the audience, there was a large picture of Jesus hanging on the back wall. I said a short prayer, knowing He would give me the words to say. Afterwards, the director of the convention came up to the stage and asked the women to gather around me, laying hands on me and to pray for my healing. I stood there for about ten minutes feeling the Holy Spirit fill the room. I then took a short break and went out in the hallway.

So many women came up to me in the hallway and restroom to tell me how much my testimony had touched their lives. Someone's sister had cancer and didn't know the Lord, so she wanted me to talk with her and encourage her; someone's mother had cancer and asked if I would pray for her; my family doctor's nurse was there and couldn't believe it was me; and many others had stories they shared with me. Several people asked me to write a book, and coincidentally, I was! We know there are no coincidences in life, so I am always amazed when God shows up like this. One person in particular told me that what amazed her the most about my testimony was that it was a living testimony. Most people will give a testimony after God answers their prayers. I was giving a testimony, believing and trusting that God would answer my prayers, and living as if He already has.

My radiation oncologist, who introduced me before I spoke, had googled my name and found that it meant illumination or light (I knew this and have always been grateful for my name, praying that God will always use me as a light for others to see Him). She wanted people to remember my name and the meaning behind it as I gave my testimony. Even though I was named by my mother and father, God put the name Lucinda in their minds, knowing full well how He would use me one day to be a light for others. I had read this in one of my devotionals, "I chose to pour My Light into you, so that you can be a beacon to others." (Young, p. 165)

I have been asked to return next year to lead a class on confidence in Christ. I pray I will still be here to fulfill that obligation. I was so filled with the Spirit while driving home. What an amazing weekend.

# Day 994 – May 9, 2018

I had round thirteen of chemo the week of May 9th. I had told Dr. E. I would go thirteen rounds before the cancer mutated! And I did. He was amazed at how well I tolerated the ifosfamide; he had never had another patient go this many rounds because it's so hard on your body. Things are getting harder and harder though, my body is wearing out and it's very taxing on both Greg and me. I'm reminded of the scripture from James 1:2-4, "Consider it pure joy whenever you face trials of many kinds, because you know that the testing of your faith produces perseverance. Let perseverance finish its work so that you may be mature and complete, not lacking anything" (*NIV*, James 1:2-4).

I had my CT scan May 22, and shortly afterwards we had some friends, Sandra and Mike, visit from Raleigh to have a few days of fun. I was able to return to my high intensity interval training classes and took them with me. My energy seemed to rebound, but it was only short-lived.

We met with Dr. E. towards the end of May to discuss the CT scan. All of my tumors were growing. The only good news was that the two tumors in my liver were gone. I still had the large tumor above my right adrenal/kidney which had grown, the one in my lymph system, and now two additional tumors—one in my right lung lobe and one near my colon on the left side. The ifosfamide was no longer effective. Dr. E. suggested a new chemo regimen unless the specialist had a silver bullet clinical trial. Chemo was cancelled the next week, and we scheduled an appointment to talk about clinical trials.

## Day 1010 – May 25, 2018


I tried to forget about my cancer and enjoyed a wonderful Memorial Day weekend with Taylor's family and some of her friends here at the lake. For me, the highlight of the weekend happened after her friends had left. Henry was so exhausted from all the weekend excitement that he curled up on the floor at Taylor's and my feet while we were relaxing in the rocking chairs on the porch. He asked me if I would sing him a song so he could go to sleep. Taylor asked him what he wanted me to sing; his response was "Bless the Lord oh my Soul." Tears just welled up in my eyes. We have been singing this song to Henry every night since his birth when we put him put down to sleep. This was the first time he had ever asked me to sing it!

After the weekend, Greg and I had our appointment with the specialist. He had a new clinical trial opening up in the summer that looked promising. It would be a phase one, but it was specifically for endometrial cancer (which is not what I have but is at least in the same area). He suggested I start the new chemo regimen Dr. E. was recommending, and hope it shrinks the tumors so that they can then pull me off the chemo to try the clinical trial.

I would prefer to enter the trial when it's in phase two, after figuring out the correct dose. The trial in phase two focuses on the effectiveness of killing the cancer. I would need to be off of chemo for about three to four weeks to clean out my system, and then hopefully I would have time for at least two cycles of the trial, each three weeks long, to see if it works. In the meantime, if it doesn't work, my tumors continue to grow rapidly. The chemo won't kill the tumors, so my only hope with chemo is to stabilize them or possibly shrink them, whereas a clinical trial drug could potentially kill the cancer.

After being a little overwhelmed with our direction moving forward (I was really wearing out from chemo), flowers showed up from my massage therapist and we received the joyful news that our new grandson was born! Always joy in the morning.

Greg and I flew out to Denver to meet our new grandson, Everette Alan. He was named Alan after both grandfathers and Everett, which means strength, in honor of me. While there, we visited the local museum and were able to see the special exhibition of the Dead Sea Scrolls. It was so interesting to see and read some of the scrolls from Genesis, Exodus, Job and Isaiah and to see the urns where they found the scrolls. This wasn't planned, it just happened, which reminds me so much of how the Lord orders our steps, even though we may make the plans.

I had another encounter with a stranger whose father had died of cancer. He told me the Spirit had told him to speak with me. I shared my cancer story with him, and he told me he would pray for me. Another "chance" meeting of God bringing people into my life at just the right time for both of us to be blessed.

Psalm 37:23-24, "The Lord makes firm (orders) the steps of the one who delights in him; though he may stumble, he will not fall, for the Lord upholds him with his hand" (*NIV*, Ps. 37:23-24).

## Day 1022 – June 6, 2018

I started my new chemo regimen, but we're beginning to run out of options. The day before I was scheduled to start the Gemzar/Carboplatin chemo, I received a call from Hillary saying that the chemo plan had changed. The insurance company would not approve Gemzar until I tried Taxotere, so the chemo regimen was changed to Taxotere/Carboplatin. This was a major stumbling block. I had already had a similar chemo combination as my frontline treatment and didn't understand why I would have to go back to this, especially since the oncologist thought that Gemzar would be the key to hopefully shrinking my tumors.

I was concerned that the insurance company was planning my treatment, but I realized I needed to trust God's ordered steps and just move forward. Again, I was focusing too much on my circumstances. In my devotions that morning I read, "God has heard your prayer and help is on the way! God never ignores the prayer of one of His own. A fervent prayer cried...or whispered...or shouted...or uttered...or even thought...by a desperate child gets the attention of the Father. He has given heed to your cry!" (YouVersion, The Bible App). And then this: "You can glory in disappointment, because God is still on the throne of your life. He is still in control. He's got this. He's got you" (YouVersion, The Bible App).

Soon after my first treatment of Taxotere/Carboplatin, Greg and I had special time with Henry when he came to stay with us by himself for two days. We played on the lake beach and in the wading pool, pulled weeds, threw rocks in the lake, and ate watermelon and popsicles. Henry did the world famous watermelon dance because he had never eaten watermelon on the rind!

Taylor and Brad came for the weekend, and we got to see Henry jump off the dock into the lake. It was a weekend filled with joy, fun and laughter.

Then we went to Atlanta shortly afterward to celebrate Henry's second birthday with dinner, drinks, dessert and dump trucks in the park! So much fun! While there, Taylor and Brad told us they were expecting another child, due in February! My heart is just so full; God has not forsaken me. He continues to show up in the valleys to give me hope.

## Day 1041 – June 25, 2018


On June 25, I had an appointment with Dr. E.; he expressed concern about my insurance company not approving the Gemzar and Carboplatin. He was concerned we were wasting time—time that I may not have. We only have three chemos left to try along with any potential clinical trials. My CA125 was up to 133, indicating the cancer was growing, which we knew. On the way home, Greg and I talked about calling the insurance company to see if there was anything we could do. I was scheduled for chemo in two days and then a CT scan two weeks later. If the scan showed continued growth, hopefully the insurance company would let us switch to Gemzar, but by that time my tumors would have been growing rapidly for eight to ten weeks.

I called my insurance company and apparently there had been a major miscommunication. Gemzar and Taxotere are the front line treatments for sarcomas, and the insurance company saw no reason why this wasn't approved. I informed Dr. E., he canceled my upcoming chemo and put in orders for the new chemo. Hopefully it could be scheduled within two days!

In the meantime, Sean, Lindsey, Cora and baby Everett came to visit us for the weekend. Unfortunately, I spent a lot of those two days on the phone, trying to get my chemo straightened out. It was getting very frustrating. I have enough to be concerned about without fighting my insurance company. As it turns out, Gemzar/Taxotere was *not* approved for carcinosarcoma specifically but for other sarcomas. I reached out to anyone I could, even my former employer through whom I am still insured. There was no way to get the drugs approved in time for my chemo, which now had to be postponed again for several days. I was extremely upset, but I put it behind me, trusting God as I moved forward. I finally had my first round of the new chemo, Gemzar, the next Tuesday and was thankful we were moving forward.

# Day 1056 – July 10, 2018

On July 10th, I had my second chemo treatment. The treatment regimen is a three week cycle: Gemzar the first week, Gemzar/Taxotere the second week, and then a week off. Having had very little reaction to the first treatment of only Gemzar, I planned to go to NYC with Taylor and Henry to help get them settled (Taylor had to be there for eight weeks of training for her new job). One of the major side effects of Gemzar is lower blood counts of red and white blood cells as well as platelets.

After I had received just the Gemzar, my platelets dropped to 89,000, and the nurse said chemo is withheld at 75,000. She had to get permission from Dr. E. to give me the Gemzar/Taxotere. It was approved, but since I was hoping to fly that weekend, Dr. E. wanted to check my blood to see how much more they would drop. Keep in mind the normal range for platelets is 125,000-400,000. Bad news: my platelets had dropped to 35,000. I was advised not to fly as the pressure on the plane could cause a vessel to rupture and I could easily hemorrhage because my blood had virtually no capacity to clot. I could get to New York without an incident, but I was not at my nadir (low point) yet, so the trip home would be even worse.

I was so sad! I was really looking forward to spending several days with Henry. I called Taylor crying and canceled my trip. It's very hard when cancer restricts you from living a normal life. I know the Lord has kept me strong for the three years I have been battling cancer, and I am grateful, but the battle continues to get harder. I am not afraid of dying and I look forward to seeing Jesus, but I just want to see my grandchildren grow up and I want to spend time with my husband and children. There is still hope, and I truly believe God is not done with me yet on this earth.

I had to get my platelets re-checked the following Monday. They had dropped to 13,000! Dr. E. wanted to check it again the next day to see if they would start to rise. On Tuesday they were at 9,000—pretty critical. I was told to go straight to the hospital. I was there for three days and received two units of platelets and three units of whole blood because my white blood count had dropped to zero. I was put on two strong antibiotics since my body was unable to fight any infection. Greg expressed concern about my bone marrow dying off, but Dr. E. said he wouldn't let that happen.

I love how God continues to put angels in my life. The night before I left the hospital, the night shift technician, Natalie, came in to see me. We both recognized each other! She had been my technician two years ago when I was in the hospital for a major infection and had missed Taylor's baby shower. She was the one who prayed over me as the nurse put an NG tube through my nose into my stomach. I told her I was writing a book and she got so . excited; she told everyone on the hospital floor!

I didn't realize how close to death I was, and I'm so grateful to have regained my strength. I was in such a critical condition that Greg had sent a text to the kids, and they had booked flights to come see me, thinking the end was near. I was very tired and needed to be cautious of germs until we knew my counts had stabilized, but it was so great to be surrounded by family, even though the grandchildren couldn't visit. Several days later I had my blood tested and all my counts were within normal range! Praise God, I have been healed once again! Time to crawl back out of the valley again. In the meantime, Greg had had a dream the night before where God spoke to him and told him my tumors were shrinking. He told me it wasn't an audible voice, but it was like someone speaking in his mind. I told him that's how God speaks to us. I told him to pay attention to that and to hang on to that hope. Another reminder that God will heal me completely.

# Day 1071 – July 25, 2018

Greg and I met with Dr. E. to discuss plans moving forward. He would like to restart my chemo the next week with the Gemzar, but he wanted to modify the regimen: lower the Gemzar dose by thirty percent, have a week to recover, then have Gemzar with Taxotere (dose decreased by twenty-five percent), and then another week to recover. He thinks a four week regimen would give my body a chance to recover better than a three week regimen.

He brought up hospice again. The last time we discussed hospice was the previous August after I had my last surgery. At that time he didn't give me much chance to live past Christmas. My cancer has progressed more now than it had then. Dr. E seemed to indicate that unless the tumors shrink or stop growing, there isn't a lot of time left. He mentioned again the two more chemos I had left to try and the possibility of a clinical trial. My CA125 was now at 150 and he could feel my large tumor. He said we were in salvage mode now, trying whatever he could to keep me alive. We could continue treatments as long as I was healthy and could tolerate the toxicity levels or until I have a complication from the growing tumors, whichever came first. It was a sobering moment, but I said, "Let's keep going...I still believe I will be healed."

## Day 1096 – August 19, 2018


I've had an unusual few weeks starting to plan my end of life celebration. After losing both of my parents, I realize what a burden it is for others to do this, especially in a time of grief. I still believe God will heal me. I know He can if it is His will. But I have also accepted that if He chooses not to heal me here on earth but rather in heaven, it will be for His greater glory, and I am okay with that. After all, I don't have a choice! If it is His will to keep me here to glorify Him, I will gladly stay, watch my grandchildren grow up, and enjoy retirement with Greg on the lake. If He chooses to bring me home, I look forward to that glorious day and pray the passing is easy.

The Lord knows my heart's desire, but He is in control. And I love that He is the one who makes those decisions. We never know what our future entails, but one thing we all know: everyone will eventually die. I may survive this incurable cancer by a miracle, but I will eventually die. My desire is to finish strong, praising God to the very end.

I met with my pastor, Blake, and I shared some of my desires for my end of life celebration with him. We laughed a lot as we discussed plans, and I left with a long list of things to do!

I finished my second complete round of Gemzar/Taxotere this past week and, praise God, my blood counts and platelets didn't drop low enough for me to be admitted to the hospital. On Saturday and Sunday my health was weakening, but I managed to make it to church on Sunday. I was sitting with my friend, Kim, when the service ended and Blake asked me to come forward. He wanted the church to pray for me, and to pray boldly and selfishly for my healing. He wanted the church to pray for shrinkage of my tumors as my next CT scan was coming in the following week. But most of all he wanted to pray for God to be glorified through my affliction, as giving God all the glory is our purpose in life. My eyes were filled with tears as people came forward and put their outstretched hands on me. God is doing a mighty work, and for this I am truly grateful.

After the service, a young man named Dave came up to me and held my hand. He had seen me several months before in church and the Holy Spirit had pressed on his heart to come speak to me. At that time he did not respond. When Blake asked the church to lay hands on me, he rushed from the back of the church and was the first to reach me, laying his hand on the back of my neck, responding obediently this time to the Spirit's prompting and knowing God can do miraculous things. We don't know why the Spirit does what He does, but our response to His promptings is so important. God will heal me, this I know. God has used too many strangers to tell me!

The next week my older brother, Vaughan, came for a visit. After my last hospital visit, John had told him that things weren't looking too good. The visit was great. We had a quiet lunch together where I shared with him how the past few weeks had been and that I was starting to plan my end of life celebration. We both shed some tears. The next day we took a long walk and I shared with him that I was okay if I died; I was at peace. The sad part is leaving those we love behind. I think now he better understands what I have been going through and I am so grateful for this special time that we had together.

# End


I have had a rare cancer for over 1000 days now (*exactly* three years August 19, 2018). At first, I had a twenty percent chance of being alive in five years. When my cancer metastasized a year ago, my prognosis got worse—I was dying. From day one, I have had hope in the Lord that I will be healed. Over 1000 days later, my story is yet unfinished.

Perhaps the most important thing is this: I haven't lost one night of sleep due to *worrying* about this cancer. God laid it on my heart when I was first diagnosed that He had this and not to worry, and I haven't worried. I know that I have no control over it. Thankfully, I know who has ultimate control: God. I've been able to have joy throughout this tragic disease because I truly know that nothing can separate me from His presence, and it is in His presence where there is always fullness of joy. Neither death nor disease are able to deny me the strength and comfort of His presence.

Since coming to know the Lord fourteen years ago, I knew my life was never meant to be ordinary nor was it meant to be mundane. I believe God has always planned for my life to be a miraculous demonstration of the power of God manifesting itself in mere mortals. The irony of our destiny is that it is rarely discerned in our lifetimes, oftentimes it's not revealed until after we die. God ordained my days and ordered my footsteps, and He did it before I was conceived.

I would not choose cancer. But God, who wastes nothing, has used this cancer for His glory. Cancer isn't easy, but the Lord's yoke is easy and His burden is light. My cancer burden is the Lord's and He is all-knowing. His plan is always better than my plan. Neither you, nor I, nor any created being has ever had a better idea than God. The Lord has taught me to be thankful for my cancer and the way that He has used it to bless others.

It is my fervent prayer that God will continue to use me, whether or not I have cancer. As Paul says in Philippians, "For to me, to live is Christ and to die is gain. If I am to go on living in the body, this will mean fruitful labor for me…I desire to depart and be with Christ, which is better by far; but it is more necessary for you that I remain in the body" (*NIV*, Phil. 1:21-24). It is God's choice and plan whether I live or die, but I believe that He is not finished with me yet. If it's His will that I live, I will continue to give Him all the praise and glory as my healing continues. After all, even with all the skill and knowledge my doctors have, those doctors are not the last word in whether I live or die. What a doctor can do is work with the body God created and the systems He put in place. The power for a drug to work in my body lies solely in the hands of God and the body He designed.

He can heal me right now; He can heal me with treatments, surgery, prayer, divine intervention or ultimate healing in heaven. It is His choice and I trust Him. I am reminded again of the woman in the Bible that was subjected to bleeding for twelve years and was healed. She had already suffered a great deal under the care of many doctors and had spent all she had, yet instead of getting better, she got worse. Jesus did not say it was wrong to go to the doctors, He accepted her faith and healed her. I, too, believe I will be healed and look forward to the next chapter in my life and what God has in store for me— whatever that may be. And in the meantime, it is well with my soul.

I dedicate the end of the book to my two year old grandson, Henry Luke, whose favorite song is "Bless the Lord"[2] or "10,000 Reasons" by Matt Redman.

Bless the Lord O my soul
O my soul
Worship His Holy name
Sing like never before
O my soul
I'll worship Your Holy name

The sun comes up
It's a new day dawning
It's time to sing Your song again
Whatever may pass
And whatever lies before me
Let me be singing
When the evening comes

You're rich in love
And You're slow to anger
Your name is great
And Your heart is kind
For all Your goodness
I will keep on singing
Ten thousand reasons
For my heart to find

And on that day
When my strength is failing
The end draws near
And my time has come
Still my soul will
Sing Your praise unending
Ten thousand years

² Redman, Matt. "10,000 Reasons (Bless The Lord)." 10,000 Reasons, 2011, track 4. Genius, https://genius.com/Matt-redman-10000-reasons-bless-the-lord-lyrics.

And then forever more

Bless the Lord O my soul
O my soul
Worship His Holy name
Sing like never before
O my soul
I'll worship Your Holy name

# ACKNOWLEDGMENTS

I wouldn't have written this book had not my daughter, Taylor, given me a journal to write my story and had not God laid it on my heart to turn the journal into a book of encouragement for others who are dealing with tragic suffering in their lives. I am grateful to Taylor for her help with this legacy of mine and for her unconditional love throughout our lives. She is truly a special daughter; I thank God for her, and I will love her forever.

I am grateful to Heather Grizzle and Samantha Swenson, with whom Taylor put me in touch. I am grateful to Samantha for all the editing she did throughout this process and to Heather for guiding me in getting this book published.

I thank God for all my prayer warriors who covered me in prayer for over three years. I would not have lived as long as I did without them. To my prayer warriors, your prayers and words of encouragement meant more to me than you will ever know. A special thank you to:

Cindy Aggers, Herbie Anderson, Katie Arnold, Debra Babcock, Becky Betts, Karen Biddy, Sandra Birckhead, Robbie and Ruthie Bolin, Brad and Annie Brown, Becky and Phil Buckhiester, Cheryl Caron, Chad Carroll, Ann Carwile, Wendy Christensen, Nicole Copen, Dottie Corey, Barbara Costa, Erin Crook, Cora Darrah, April Davis, Courtney Day, Kristin DeCou, Charlene Dennen, Bob and MaryAnn Doherty, Jeff and Pat Doherty, Sean and Lindsey Doherty, Nicole Doherty, Kathy Emmons, Kristi Ferrel, Marlene Fitzgerald, Essie Fletcher, Parker Flowers, Terry Foil, Kathy Forse, Robin Foss, Rhonda Garrett, Sally Glynn, Shannon Goodman, Karen Hartney, Ann Hemphill, Diane Henry, Dick Henry, Sabrina Henry-King, Wendy Hicks, Bob and Sue Hove, Dick and

Anita Hudgins, Cheryl Hunter, Tim and Jody Jackson, Myra and Murray Jolly, Francis and Lydiah Katiba, Alicia Keys, Kaye King, Jennifer Kirby, Chris Koppen, Tara Lavoie, Lynda Leard, Trevor and Sarah Locklear, Jud and Denise Lusk, Kay and Max MacDonald, Crissty Martin, Shirnette Matthews, Ann Mcgrew, Jan Mckinney, Brad and Taylor Meyer, Ted and Gail Meyer, Bill and Beth Miller, Isaiah and Karin Monrose, Tricia Monteith, Maureen Moynihan, Teresia Muthoni, Carolyn Nalley, Gigi Nelson, Kim Newton, Ruth Nyambura, Terri O'Barr, Tiffany Oettinger, Brooke Olinger, John and Rhonda Olinger, Maddison Olinger, Mary Frances Olinger (deceased), Vaughan Olinger, Alice O'Neal (deceased), Dave O'Neal, Susan O'Neal, Marie Page, Jill Perez, Beth Pitton-August, Blake Pitts, Bobby and Martha Poston, Kimberly Poteat, Judy Price, Pam Rogers, Billie Sanders, Adrian and Nemanja Savic, Mark and Brooke Schmidt, Brenda Shaver, Shabina Sheikh, Pegye Skelton, Linda Skene, Mich Sturley, Phil Szostak, Jeff Tennant, Susan Tennant (deceased), Nan Thompson, Debbie Thurman, Keri Unsworth, Tony Vincent, Cindy Wawro, Kathy Westerman, Cheryl Williams, Ryan Wilson and Bonnie Yoder.

I would also like to thank spouses, family members and friends who are not listed above, as I know my prayer requests were shared with others. I would like to thank Trinity Baptist Church, LifePoint Church, and all of their members for their prayers. I am thankful for my LifePoint small group that always covered me in prayer, along with the women's Bible study group from Trinity.

My story traveled throughout the United States—across North and South Carolina, as far north as New York and west to California—and even to far parts of the world, in Europe and Africa. I am grateful for prayers from the people with whom I shared my story as well as prayers from people I don't know. You have all been a part of this story.

I am grateful to Greenville Health System and their incredible oncology department as well as all the doctors and nurses who have kept me alive with the help of God, who truly deserves all credit and glory.

I would like to thank Tara Lavoie of Blossoming Soul Yoga, Jan McKinney of Healing Touch by Jan, and Bobby Campbell of Extreme Fitness for help with my physical well-being. As God was doing His part, I needed to do mine.

I am grateful to my brother, John, and and his wife, Rhonda Olinger, who have always been there for me. Not a week went by that they didn't check on me, and when times were bad, they were here.

Last but most importantly, I am grateful for my immediate family: my daughter, Taylor, her husband, Brad, and their son, Henry; Greg's son, Sean, his wife, Lindsey, and their children, Cora and Everett; and Greg's daughter, Nicole. They spent many days visiting and helping take care of me. Their love and support means more to me than they will ever know.

I will forever be grateful to my husband, Greg, who enjoyed the good times and endured the really hard times throughout this cancer. His patience grew as he repeated over and over again all the things I forgot because of chemo brain. His heart softened as I grew weaker. He tended to my everyday issues with a smile, a joke and, at times, a laugh. He loved me...and he always made me coffee. My love forever to Greg.

Proceeds of the sale of "God Shows Up in the Valleys: My Personal Journey with an Incurable Cancer," by Lucinda Doherty, will be donated to the GHS Cancer Institute in Greenville, South Carolina to support cancer research of rare tumors. Lucinda was treated at GHS and participated in several of their clinical trials.

# SOURCES & END NOTES

Peterson, Eugene H. *The Message: The Bible in Contemporary Language*. Colorado Springs: NavPress, 2002. Print.

*The Holy Bible: New International Version*. Zondervan, 1984.

*The English Standard Version Bible*. New York: Oxford University Press, 2009. Print.

Young, Sarah. *Jesus Calling: Enjoying Peace in His Presence*. Tennessee, Thomas Nelson, 2004.

Chambers, Oswald. *My Utmost for His Highest*. Dodd, Mead & Co., 1995.

Cowman, L. B. *Streams in the Desert*. Zondervan, 1997.

MercyMe. "Even If." *Lifer*, 2017, track 5. *Genius*, genius.com/Mercyme-even-if-lyrics.

Redman, Matt. "10,000 Reasons (Bless The Lord)." *10,000 Reasons*, 2011, track 4. *Genius*, https://genius.com/Matt-redman-10000-reasons-bless-the-lord-lyrics.

Made in the USA
Columbia, SC
19 September 2019